ORGANIZATIONAL
BEHAVIOR MANAGEMENT

A PRACTITIONER'S GUIDE TO MAKING A POSITIVE DIFFERENCE

MANUEL "MANNY" RODRIGUEZ, DBA, BCBA

Bueno Ventures, Inc. Miami, Florida, U.S.A.

Organizational Behavior Management: A Practitioner's Guide To Making A Positive Difference. 2021. First Edition, 305 Publishing: Miami, FL. USA.

First Printing: 2021
ISBN

Bueno Ventures, Inc.
8240 Northwest 52nd Terrace
Suite 202
Doral, FL 33166
info@buenoventures.com

ACKNOWLEDGEMENTS

Over the years I have had the great honor and opportunity to work with some amazing professionals. As a twenty something year old I had the chance of a lifetime to work with the people at Aubrey Daniels International, spending time with Aubrey Daniels himself, Darnell Lattal, Ken Wagner, David Uhl, Jamie Daniels, and Judy Agnew who provided so many valuable learning opportunities. Following this steppingstone came seven years working as a consultant with The Continuous Learning Group, now called Alula. Leslie Braksick, Julie Smith, Ned Morse, Steve Jacobs, Brian Cole, Kathy Callahan, the late Jim Hillgren. Tracy Thurkow, Charles Carnes, Travis McNeal, Carolina Aguilera, Judy Johnson, Stephen Quenelle, Heinz Buschang, Bob Foxworthy, Laura Methot and Courtney Mills shaped my consulting practice and skill sets in every way.

I took a corporate job with FMC Corporation and learned a great deal from EHS professionals Alfred Kobylinski, Michelle Brown, Randall Leathers, the late John Bell, and the EHS Managers across the company. My mentor and boss, Humberto Caldelas, was central to my growth as a manager and executive, as was our VP of Operations, Barry Crawford. My life came full circle in the last five years, and I owe much of my current success to the late Jose Martinez-Diaz, Tom Freeman, Kristin Meyers-Kemp, Alicia Norris, and Darnell Lattal (the very same from my Aubrey Daniels International days). They introduced me to the world of online learning and behavior analysis applied to higher education. I owe them a great deal. We had many successes together, however on a personal note I made some poor choices while working with them. I have corrected my behavior, my path and journey as a practitioner, and I am forever grateful for their courage to shining a light on my behavior so I can make the right choices moving forward.

This led to my more recent years as a practitioner and my final acknowledgements – Bueno Ventures, my DBA cohort, and Trenton Corporation. I found a true business partner in Adam Ventura. Together we created Bueno Ventures Management Services. In doing so I have begun fulfilling my lifelong dreams of bringing OBM to the world in various ways. I have learned a great deal from those who have partnered with Adam and I. Janet Vasquez, Natalie Parks, Yendri Diaz, Brian Conners, our clients, and last but certainly not least Adam himself. During this same time, I was able to form a group of practitioners who further educated me on the practice of OBM. Barbara Bucklin, Leah Fennema Hall, Julie Eshleman, Shane Isley, Alicia Parr, Kyle Ditzian, Amanda Barnett, Emily Gale Moses, and Edward Blackman.

Over the years I have had the pleasure to learn from and work with many OBM practitioners, researchers, and educators. The list is extensive, but I would be remised not to acknowledge the following individuals who have shaped my behavior as a practitioner in more ways than one. Jon Bailey, Tim Ludwig, Roger Addison, Roger Kaufman, Alicia Alvero, Heather McGee, Don Hantula, Cloyd Hyten, John Austin, Nicole Gravina, Howard Lees, Jeanine Stratton, Tom Mawhinney, Alice Dickinson, Florence DiGennarro Reed, Paul Fjelsta, Nic Weatherly, Paul Gavoni, and Brett DiNovi.

During our startup years I was pursuing the Doctorate of Business Administration at the University of South Florida Muma College of Business. I have been inspired by my cohort, academics, executives, and leaders in the military have given me a wealth of knowledge beyond the outstanding curriculum we got to experience. Along with my cohort were the professors and my dissertation committee who inspired me greatly.

Lastly, I want to acknowledge my colleagues at Trenton Corporation, who have provided me with an opportunity to practice OBM and make a positive difference every day. The Kennedy family who owns and leads our organization, and the operations team I get to work with every day.

Finally, I wish to acknowledge all those who call themselves OBM practitioners. The work world is a better place because of you, and my hopes and dreams are to support to growth of our field. Thank you, to all of you, who have shaped my behavior, helped me, supported me, provided consequences to me to do and be better, and to those reading this book...thank you for being part of the future of OBM.

Manny

CONTENTS

INTRODUCTION

Professionals around the world have dedicated their practice to making a positive difference in the workplace using a science-based approach unlike any other—organizational behavior management (OBM). With deep roots in industrial engineering and behaviorism, OBM tackles business-world challenges with precision and focus to help organizations achieve superior performance.

In a world where businesses are growing, merging, producing products faster and leaner than ever before, and talent is developed through innovative learning techniques, the needs of managers to ensure successful performance management is greater than ever. Since the early 70's, OBM has fostered applied and laboratory research to study human dynamics in the workplace, solving problems in areas such as safety, productivity, customer service, quality, process improvement, training and development, revenue and profitability, and employee satisfaction. Grounded by the concepts and principles of behavior analysis, evolving the core theorems from industrial engineering and business, and focusing on application to solving socially significant business needs, the OBM practitioner has become a vital member of organizations worldwide.

This book is dedicated to the individuals who call themselves OBM practitioners, scientists, researchers, entrepreneurs, and students. It is a book several years in the making as I have grown as a scientist-practitioner, entrepreneur, educator, and a forever student. With over twenty years of experience, multiple mentors who are gurus in the field, and learning from colleagues and clients alike, I am honored to have had the opportunity to write this book. I have organized the book to ensure some core concepts, principles, and application methodologies are covered. Unlike other books, **I focused here on the practitioner**.

Each chapter includes various concepts and principles of obm, examples, and we go beyond the basics to ensure the reader gains a whole perspective of what it means to be an OBM practitioner. The end of this book tackles ethics and the OBM practitioner and includes ethical guidelines for the OBM practitioner. I admit I have made my fair share of poor choices. I have learned from those choices, the impact they had on others, and thanks to mentors, colleagues, and dear friends, I have grown professionally and personally. Writing these ethical guidelines for OBM practitioners is to support the practitioner being ethical, thinking through their role, and protecting others. The role of an OBM practitioner is quite simple yet complicated in practice – making a positive difference in the workplace. That is what we do, that is why we do what we do, and we can make a difference.

OBM... WHAT'S THAT?

Photo by Anna Shvets from Pexels

Organizational behavior management (OBM) encompasses the study and practice of human behavior in business settings. The objective of OBM can be summarized as follows:

- to solve problems,
- to solve those problems with a laser focus on human behavior and the organizational systems,
- to engage people in the process of change, and
- to show measurable progress over time, leading to sustainable improvement and a return on investment.

Practitioners and researchers alike have worked with organizations large and small to unleash the power of this science. From startups looking to increase the number of customers they serve and their overall revenue, to Fortune 100 companies going through mergers and acquisitions, something unifies all organizations to achieve those desired outcomes—human behavior.

By scientifically understanding human behavior, especially how to positively influence human behavior in the business setting, supervisors, managers, executives, and investors alike have seen accelerated returns.

So how did this field originate? It all started in the 1970s (Dickinson, 2000) when practitioners and researchers came together from the field of applied behavior analysis (ABA), a specialty drawn from the philosophical foundation of behaviorism. By focusing on human behavior, these practitioners worked with organizations far and wide to demonstrate measurable value. The OBM pioneers had worked in a variety of industries and were educated in areas such as psychology, organizational behavior, industrial engineering, mental health, and business, among other areas. After many years of working together, these leaders united to bring about a single focus: to educate, disseminate, and grow the science of human behavior applied to the business world, namely OBM.

Of course, OBM has a foundation which it was built upon prior to the formal creation. The foundation can be summarized in four parts: behaviorism, behavior analysis, industrial engineering, and psychology.

For our purposes, behaviorism and ABA will be paired together. *Behaviorism* is a learning theory based on the idea that all behaviors are acquired through interactions with the environment. In other words, behaviorists believe that our responses to environmental stimuli shape our actions. As a psychological approach, behaviorism emphasizes scientific and objective methods of investigation, one focused only on observable stimulus–response behaviors. Most of you have likely heard of John B. Watson, the father of behaviorism. But B.F Skinner, considered the father of radical behaviorism, then extended Watson's work to include inner physiological processes.

So how does this all relate to OBM? In *Science and Human Behavior*, Skinner (1953) discussed economic control in regard to influencing behavior—from wage schedules to differential reinforcement of quality of work, to economics. This early work helped establish the foundation of behaviorism and its focus on the dynamics of workplace behavior. Although Skinner was not the first to explore workplace behavior in the context of behaviorism and behavior analysis, the work was truly pioneering. That shifts the focus to ABA, which is the applied study and practice of behaviorism, and how it supports the world by offering a positive means of behavior change.

Also relevant to the workplace is *industrial engineering* (Dickinson, 2000), which is the study and practice of optimizing complex processes and systems by developing, improving, and implementing integrated systems of people, money, knowledge, information, equipment, energy, and materials. Industrial engineers apply science to solve complex issues, a perfect foundation for OBM.

It was Frederick W. Taylor (1856–1915) who led the development of industrial engineering as a discipline. Taylor is well-known for his *principles of scientific management* and published a book with the same title in 1911. Based on these principles, Taylor discusses how to save time and money when laborers work to their utmost capabilities. The fundamental principles that Taylor saw underlying the scientific approach to management are summarized as follows:

1. *Replace rule-of-thumb work methods with methods based on a scientific study of the tasks.*
2. *Scientifically select, train, and develop each worker rather than passively leaving workers to train themselves.*
3. *Cooperate with workers to ensure the scientifically developed methods are being followed.*
4. *Divide work nearly equally between managers and workers, ensuring managers apply scientific management principles to planning the work and workers perform the tasks.*

As for psychology, it is a broad field of study and practice in and of itself and lends a great deal to the field of OBM. Business psychology, social psychology, and industrial/organizational psychology are all sub-fields of psychology that have been studied and compared to OBM. Each of these sub-fields deserves standalone courses for one to study, and a great deal of opportunities certainly exist to independently study these areas. For the purposes of our introduction to OBM, however, we simply want to acknowledge these fields have majorly influenced the current state of OBM.

Given the wide-ranging influences that have shaped the science, crafting a comprehensive introduction to OBM is quite a feat. One main component must be stressed from the beginning, however: OBM is a scientific approach to improving business. OBM professionals ultimately seek to solve problems. To do so scientifically, practitioners must employ the scientific method, as outlined below:

- identify and define the problem,
- measure the problem,
- analyze the problem,
- determine and implement a solution to the problem,
- evaluate the solution in relation to the defined problem, and
- determine whether success criteria or the early hypothesis were met and, if so, how to maintain the progress.

OBM practitioners, just like any other practitioner, may not use scientific jargon. In fact, doing so is discouraged, mainly to avoid distracting from the main point—OBM works, and it is a science. Practitioners typically use a more universally accepted means of sharing the process of OBM, something like a stream of who, what, when, where, why and how questions:

> This rigorous approach to problem-solving is what makes OBM so unique, so special, and so scientific.

What is the problem? Why is it a problem? What is the desired situation? How did it become a problem? How do we measure it? What solutions could be implemented? Who would be involved? How do we know the problem has been solved?

This stream of questions may seem daunting at first, but from a scientific perspective, the questions are essential to solving the problem. Even more importantly, the questions ensure practitioners have a full picture of the problem and potential solutions to resolve the problem. Practitioners and researchers alike use questions and direct observation to determine the best course of action.

Indeed, it is by meeting and asking questions of key stakeholders in an organization, from top executives to front-line employees, that the OBM practitioner garners a true understanding, a detailed account, and a direct perspective from the people directly involved with the problem and potential solutions. This rigorous approach to problem-solving is what makes OBM so unique, so special, and so scientific.

Today, OBM is a rapidly growing field, with practitioners and researchers all over the globe, focusing on the application and demonstration of the science across a variety of industries—health care, chemical manufacturing, technology, finance, human services, education, food manufacturing, telecommunications, and hospitality. Each year, these practitioners and researchers reunite at professional conferences, engage through social networking, and write in various journals and magazines to continue the same mission as the early pioneers in the 1970s.

You may be wondering how OBM is different from other approaches to performance improvement? In short, **OBM is fundamentally focused on human behavior and applying scientific rigor. No constructs. No personality types. No conceptual or hypothetical guessing. OBM simply uses the power of direct observation, data collection, and targeted solutions based on analysis to effect and sustain positive change**. Many other disciplines claim to use science because they use direct observations, interview stakeholders, and so on. However, the result—meaning the solutions these other disciplines implement—tends to be more conceptual, ambiguous, and vague. The result also often has little to no empirical research to support the solutions. In short, the results are not very scientific, making it hard to prove a solution will work or even validate its effectiveness.

Now, that's not to say OBM doesn't have great similarities to other disciplines—in fact, OBM *does* relate strongly to a number of other fields, such as industrial engineering, industrial/organizational psychology, and human performance technology. But the difference between OBM and these similar fields is three-fold: (a) OBM focuses on individuals, teams, processes, and organizational layers versus just one or a few of these; (b) OBM includes direct observation of behavior each and every time; and (c) OBM measures behavior and the business outcomes collectively rather than independently.

And now just one little additional bit of history about OBM—it is no cookie-cutter solution or flavor of the month. How do we know? Well, it is based on the scientific method. The solutions applied are therefore all based on two things: analysis and empirically validated solutions and/or grounded concepts and principles of human behavior. This approach to solutions is key because other fields apply the boxed solution, an *off-the-shelf solution* as some would phrase it, and the one-size-fits-all approach to organizational change and behavior change. As OBM practitioners, we say no to these approaches because they simply do not work.

Before moving to the next section, we wanted to pay tribute to pioneers in the field of OBM. These individuals helped OBM get started and created the influence of our chosen title, while others started a movement in the 21st century to bring OBM to a more mainstream audience. These starters of OBM deserve far more attention and attribution than we can provide. Indeed, these individuals have contributed a great deal to the field, and we hope you take the time to read their works on your own while striving to continuously develop your skills as an OBM professional.

THE OBJECTIVES OF OBM

Organizational behavior management (OBM) is a field of study and practice of human behavior in business settings. The objective of OBM can be summarized as follows:

- to solve problems organizations face
- to solve those problems with a laser focus on human behavior and the organizational systems
- to engage people in the process of change
- to measurably show progress over time leading to sustainable improvement and return on investment.

What experience at this point do you have with OBM? What other approaches have you seen companies use to meet the same or similar objectives?

IN YOUR OWN WORDS, DESCRIBE THE SCIENTIFIC METHOD AS IT APPLIES TO OBM.

Identify and define the problem
Measure the problem
Analyze the problem
Determine and implement a solution to the problem
Evaluate the solution in relation to the defined problem
Determine if success criteria or the early hypothesis was met and is so how to maintain the progress

THE DIFFERENTIATORS OF OBM: CAN YOU THINK OF OTHERS?

1. OBM focuses on individuals, teams, processes, and organizational layers versus just one or a few of these;
2. OBM includes direct observation of behavior each and every time;
3. OBM measures behavior and the business outcomes collectively not independently.

Yours thoughts here of other differentiators of OBM:

BUSINESS IS BEHAVIOR

Photo by Lilli Waugh from Pexels

It should be of no surprise that business simply does not happen unless people behave. Now, this does not mean only good behavior. Rather, simply put, if people didn't walk, talk, sell, review customer orders, track hours, deliver products, and so on...if these behaviors didn't happen, companies would fail. An understanding of human behavior is therefore critical for the success of any business.

This premise is the very foundation of OBM, a study and supportive science of human behavior with the aim to maximize business outcomes.

Behavior is what you see, what you hear, and even your own thoughts. Every day, people do something at work. People answer phone calls and emails to interact with customers, vendors, and colleagues. Attend meetings to gather new information and make decisions. Facilitate training, whether in the classroom or on the job. Create new innovative products. Operate and maintain critical equipment that produces products. As you can see by these examples, behavior is the difference between success in business and no business at all.

To truly understand behavior, you must first know what influences behavior. To start, history—specifically an individual's learning history—influences behavior. What they learned as children, as young adults, and as employees of organizations creates a great learning history of what behavior is acceptable and rewarded versus what behavior is punished and deemed inappropriate. One's learning history is unique, although some similarities may exist from one person to another. Every supervisor, manager, or executive would be served well to learn their people's individual learning histories.

Here, such history refers not to values or morals, but rather speaks to what behaviors individuals have learned are acceptable and desirable behavior. Imagine a call center representative answering phones all day. In their day to day, they answer the phone and are direct, monotone, and unapologetic to the customers if something happened with their orders. At some point, this individual learned this behavior was okay, acceptable, and desired. Would it be for you? Most would say "no," that the desirable behavior would be using a courteous, friendly tone and being apologetic if something occurred to the customer's dissatisfaction.

Thus, learning about an individual's learning history allows you to take an active role in making any needed changes to more desirable behaviors. In short, if you know about people's past histories, then you can coach and mentor toward a positive future.

Another major influence in the workplace is organizational systems. What are those? Organizational systems comprise the mission, vision, values, policies, procedures, rules (written and unwritten), even daily orders that typically change from one day to the next. Each of these systems influence human behavior—what people do, why they do it, and how they do it are all driven by various organizational systems.

One clear example can be found in the telecommunications industry. As a customer, you experience several organizational systems from which employees work. The enrollment process, fee structure, cancellation policies, late fees, and even getting upgrades are all based on the organization's policies and procedures. If you have ever changed telecommunication providers, you may have also recognized a difference from one company to the next—not all companies have the same systems guiding employee behavior. In a way, organizational systems are arguably a differentiator, a competitive edge for an organization; the one with the best systems may in fact cultivate the best behaviors. But organizational systems alone do not influence behavior.

Accomplishments are the immediate experiences a person has after doing a behavior. Consider what you do every day. Do you interact with customers? Check inventory? Calibrate process equipment? Make sales calls? Every day you work, hopefully productively, and feel accomplished. You completed some things on your to-do list. You made a call to a prospective client. A client gave you positive feedback. Nothing bad happened—hey, that is an accomplishment. In every instance of behavior, you're working to accomplish something. Those accomplishments add up to outcomes. Not every call ends with a sale. Not every customer interaction is a positive one. Not every time you check on critical process equipment is there no issue. The end results are clear, but the behaviors you engage in are rewarded by what you accomplish along the way. It is such accomplishments that motivate people to engage in the "right" behavior.

The world of business requires a focus on behavior, but not just any behavior. There must be focus on value-adding behavior that achieves those accomplishments that then lead to business results. But what are value-adding behaviors? The answer lies in the OBM basics.

OBM Basics

Photo by Ylanite Koppens from Pexels

What do an OBM practitioner, an entrepreneur, an executive, and a student learning OBM all have in common? The basics! Whether you take a university course, complete an online webinar, or even read this book, all three will cover the basics of OBM so that every OBM practitioner or consumer of OBM will have the same foundation. Let us cover the eight basic elements of OBM, starting with behavior!

Behavior is anything a person says or does. Every day that people behave, thousands and thousands of behaviors make up the activities of a person's daily regimen. Waking up, eating, walking, talking to a customer, handling a complaint, selling a product, and making decisions form an example daily ritual of various behaviors. Without people behaving, business results don't happen. The same is true for the wrong behavior—if people are engaging in undesirable behavior, the chances of getting those business results are slim to none. It probably makes sense why OBM focuses on behavior at this point, but how do you focus on behavior?

In every organization, there are policies and procedures, checklists, and training aides, and in some organizations, the daily orders. Each of these things point to value-adding behaviors, those behaviors that are either those absolutely required (think safety) or those desired to maximize business results and customer satisfaction. If these behaviors did not happen, businesses would eventually shut down. A focus on behavior helps the organization thrive. The words people say, the actions people engage in, and the conditions within which these behaviors occur are designed by the very people who work at the organization—employees, supervisors, managers, and executives alike.

For the OBM practitioner, to maximize results, focus everyone's attention on what really matters out of all the behaviors one could engage in, you must pinpoint behaviors!

Daniels and Bailey (2014) defined pinpoints as follows:

- **A behavior or result:** A behavior consists of someone's actions while a result is what is left when the behavior is completed.
- **Measurable:** The behavior or result can be counted as occurring or existing.
- **Observable**: The behavior or result can be seen by an observer.
- **Reliable**: Two independent observers agree.
- **Active**: Passes the dead man's test.
- **Under the performer's control:** Performer must have major influence on changing the result.

Is poor communication a good pinpoint?

- NO!
  - It would be difficult to measure.
  - Difficult for two independent observers to agree.

Behavior is everything a person does.

- Good vs. bad
- Productive vs. unproductive
- Significant vs. trivial

Because behavior can be counted (meaning measured), it has value to organization.

Behaviors	Results
• Mopping the floor	• Clean office
• Data entry (typing)	• Final document
• Greeting a customer	• Meeting a customer need
• Upselling a larger soda size	• Completed sale
• Painting a house	• Painted room
• Shoveling snow	• Safe sidewalk conditions

Pinpoints become the very foundation of everything an OBM practitioner does. Once pinpoints are identified, we move towards understand the reason why people do what they do, or why people don't do what 'ought to be done. You should understand three things about behavior in the workplace:

There is always more than one set of behaviors worth focusing on, that's why we pinpoint.

Something happens before you behave (Antecedents).

Something happens after you behave (Consequences).

What Comes Before Behavior?

Every day, you perform hundreds to thousands of behaviors. You do and say things to make things happen—waking up in the morning, showering, saying good morning to loved ones and colleagues, and of course, engaging in work activities from the moment you get settled into the job for the day. These behaviors do not happen accidently. Your history of experiences, learning history if you will, and your present situations are all engineered in a way to encourage you to behave in certain ways. Whether you set an alarm clock or not, whether you stay up late or get a full night's sleep, and whether that coffee pot was set up the night before could all be encouraging or discouraging you to wake up and feel refreshed.

On the job, a prioritized list of activities to accomplish for the day versus tackling one issue after another may be the difference between you feeling successful or not. The setup of everything you do is known in behavior science as antecedents, the very triggers or history of learning that encourage or discourage your behavior. You can add new antecedents to initiate new behavior, say a new to-do item or a goal, or you can remove an antecedent that is not working for you by, for instance, reprioritizing your workload or setting a new alarm clock that actually works.

Antecedents are essential to behavior getting started, but as behavior science has shown time and time again for decades, antecedents are not sufficient to keep behavior going. You see, a to-do list, an alarm clock, or even a job you really love must all be associated with great experiences, accomplishments, or results—namely what happens after behavior.

What Happens After Behavior?

Accomplishments, goals achieved, recognition, rewards, new positive experiences, and more are all experiences that happen after behavior happens, and in behavior science, these happenings are called *consequences*. Scientifically speaking, a consequence is what comes after behavior; it is not intended to be negative or positive as consequences can be either or both, depending on the context. It is these experiences that maintain behavior, establish people's learning histories of what they will more than likely do in the future, or not do, given the consequence.

In short, consequences are the guide to future behavior. If you are recognized for doing good work, accomplishing a goal, and achieving an ultimate business result, the very behaviors that you did to achieve those positive experiences will most likely be repeated. Now, if an experience is negative, say you do not like recognition in public or you get reprimanded, the same is true—negative experiences will discourage you to do those same behaviors again in the future.

It should come as no surprise then that, with respect to behavior in the workplace, an understanding and appreciation of both antecedents and consequences become the very differentiator between success and failure. If the right antecedents are in place (policies, procedures, priorities) and there are consequences to encourage value-adding behavior (recognition, rewards), those value-adding behaviors will most likely happen again, and again, and…you get the point.

Whose Behaviors Should Be Focused On?

All too often, organizations focus on the behavior of their employees. What do employees at the front line need to do differently to improve results? It's a good starting point, and essential really for bottom-line business outcomes to be achieved, but let's face it, that question alone isn't not enough. In the workplace, employee behavior needs to be supported with leadership behavior.

We do not use the term *leadership* loosely here. Leadership is any position where someone has accountability to lead others to achieve. Trainers, HR business partners, supervisors, managers, directors, executives, and even the front desk administrative assistant you see every day all play a leadership role in the company. Employees must perform value-adding behaviors, yet the antecedents and consequences to these individuals are largely provided by organizational leaders. Policies and procedures are typically set by a corporate department head and their team. Training is provided by a training department. Resources such as equipment, uniforms, and even employee paperwork are managed and provided by support staff. These antecedents are critical to the employee's success and require those in leadership roles to be productive and supportive. In addition, leaders provide the consequences—from rewards and recognition to promotions and ongoing feedback, to employee performance. The consequences provided by leaders are vital to whether value-adding behaviors actually happen.

For the OBM practitioner, a clear understanding of antecedents and consequences is paramount to the success of the OBM strategy. Practitioners are looking to encourage value-adding behavior after all. Thus, knowing what antecedents are in place, what consequences the individuals are experiencing, and what is not in place that could further support improvement is where the OBM practitioner starts. By observing what is happening, what should be happening, and what's in effect to encourage or discourage the value-adding behavior in real time, the OBM strategy takes form to develop solutions to fully realize the behaviors, those positive accomplishments, and of course, the business outcomes.

What Is the Value of Data in OBM?

In business, data is needed to make informed decisions about the state of things. Revenue, projections, expenses, and other key indicators provide abundant information for decision-making. When it comes to performance improvement, waiting on outcomes simply is not enough. OBM teaches us the very important aspect of gathering data on the value-adding behaviors, the accomplishments, and of course, the outcomes. Notice the "and" in that statement. Data collection can be time consuming but guessing and hoping for outcomes to be achieved can be equally time-consuming and frustrating. After all, it is a bit of a waiting game. Collecting data on the value-adding behaviors that your OBM strategy is focusing on gives you a leading indication of the likelihood of reaching those desired goals—regardless of whether the individuals are experiencing those accomplishments—and how close you might get to reaching the desired business outcomes.

Imagine a sales organization focusing on, well, sales of course. Several salespeople are meeting with potential customers, following up on leads, and generating new leads through cold calls. Days and weeks go by, and no sales. The month-end has been realized with minimum sales, and the goals are not being met. What happened? The organization more than likely measured sales each day and each week and saw the end of month coming a week or more ahead. More than likely, the sales managers and director assumed two things: (a) the salespeople knew what to do to land a sale, and (b) the salespeople were self-managing their own sales behaviors. Bad assumptions. In most cases, performance, when left to chance—meaning not measured and analyzed—can surely be counted on to not happen. OBM professionals don't take such chances. Measuring those value-adding behaviors, the accomplishments experienced, and those outcomes as a collection of data is absolutely key to knowing and assuring your OBM strategy is working.

Word of caution here, though: data tracking can be complicated, time-consuming, and downright annoying for those gathering all the data. In most cases, organizations are not sophisticated with automated data-tracking systems. The data gathered is manually intensive and gathered by multiple people, leading to problems of validity. Not to mention, the data can be jeopardized if there are too many negative consequences for data gatherers and the performers themselves. Thus, make the data collection process simple, realistic, and meaningful for the OBM strategy so that you have the information needed to make informed decisions.

OBM practitioners often employ scorecards to gather all the data needed for analyzing the OBM strategy. At the point of this book writing, the balanced scorecard is not a novel tool for organizations (see Kaplan & Norton, 1992). Scorecards are organized to keep all key indicators in one place so that you can evaluate overall progress on multiple elements, from the value-adding behaviors, accomplishments, and outcomes to indicators the organization is concerned may get impacted inadvertently from the OBM strategy.

An example of this is a focus on Accounts Receivables, collections in short, and clients being contacted to pay their bills. The scorecard would have the dollars collected (outcome), the average age of accounts with overdue payments (accomplishments), and the number of clients contacted as an example (value added behavior). But customer retention/attrition would also be a vital measure to track. If customers are paying their bills but then leaving for a competitor, how can you claim the OBM strategy is successful? In short, you cannot! This example raises the important role that organizational systems play in OBM strategies.

What Role Do Organizational Systems Play?

Photo by Rodolfo Clix from Pexels

Organizational systems are the processes and procedures that hold all employees accountable. This concept may seem bureaucratic but consider the area of environmental health and safety. Organizational systems such as internal auditing protect employees and the company, ensuring safety and environmental compliance and beyond compliance is in check. Without such systems, the organization would have neither the assurance nor the direct observation-based data needed to validate such assurance.

A systems approach to performance has three main distinctions (Hyten, 2009). First, the "big picture" of the organization provides a starting point for solving the most pressing problems for the organization, avoiding menial or trivial behavior change. Second, every organizational system has subsystems, and a systems approach examines how every piece of the organization's puzzle works in conjunction with one another, avoiding unintentional issues. Third, beyond antecedents and consequences for individual performance problems, a systems approach aims to identify solutions that cut across departments, processes, and even business units. These three main distinctions are the basis for the total performance system developed by Dr. Dale Brethower (1972, 1982, 1995, 2001; Brethower & Dans,

1999). Dr. Brethower's total performance system provides a model for looking at organizational systems, summarized as follows:

- Given the organization's mission and goals, there are corresponding processing systems and receiving systems.
- Inputs exist to support the processing systems.
- Outputs of the processing systems are the inputs for the receiving systems.
- Each system has a feedback loop from internal employees (processing systems) and external sources (receiving systems).

In addition to Brethower's model, Dr. Cloyd Hyten (2009) provided the performance driver system, illustrating major elements to a management system within a company looking to improve and maintain positive performance. To achieve performance goals, Hyten described the following performance drivers:

- Goals and strategies
- Hiring practices
- Training and performance support
- Contingencies (antecedents and consequences)
- Measurement systems
- Feedback systems
- Management practices
- Resources
- Processes

By taking a systems approach, managers and OBM practitioners alike are stewarding for maximum performance improvement, solving the big problems, and attending to both the "big picture" and individual needs.

What More Is There to Learn About Performance Feedback?

Photo by Ann H from Pexels

In the field of OBM, no one topic is more researched or written about than performance feedback. In short, feedback is information given to an individual with an intent to help, not harm. Feedback is an essential part of the OBM practitioner and manager tool belt. In the workplace, feedback has been one of the most heavily influential solutions to make a positive difference for individuals, teams, and large business units to achieve. We will describe some main elements on the topic of performance feedback. However, since so much is written and researched on the topic, please consider this only your OBM start on feedback.

First, feedback is intended to help, not harm. This premise is critical as the intention of feedback for every individual in the workplace should be to help others be successful. Even the dreaded negative or constructive feedback has a positive intention—namely to be constructive so that the person can modify and adjust and be successful again in the long run. In your feedback practice, check your intentions before starting. Are you sincere and genuine in your intention to help? Can you deliver the feedback in a way that openly expresses your intention to be helpful? Do you have any hidden motives that could be "viewed" in your words or body language? Check your intentions.

Second, feedback delivery is multi-faceted. Sooner rather than later is best, but giving feedback is important versus avoiding it. Who provides the feedback is another variable; if the recipient does not respect or trust you, then it won't matter whether you are a colleague, consultant, or the boss—whatever the feedback, it won't make a bit of difference. The information being provided is also critical. Written feedback, graphic feedback, individual versus group feedback, and the amount of information all play a specific role in the person's ability to consume and act on the feedback. Finally, how often the feedback is followed up by recognition of progress and/or accomplishments is key. After giving any feedback, specifically constructive, be sure to follow up and when they do it right, give positive feedback.

Value-adding behaviors are the critical few behaviors that matter at the end of each day. Did I make those sales calls? Did I use the skills I was taught to have positive interactions with clients? Did I handle issues to a positive end? Did I get those to-dos-to-be done? What you do each day, the very behaviors you engage in, can be the difference between a productive day and a busy day. A productive day leads to various accomplishments and, ultimately, to those business outcomes. A busy day, well, everyone has had those days. Nothing got done. You don't feel accomplished. That to-do list grew with more to-dos. A productive day is the very evidence of engaging in value-adding behaviors.

So how does one define value-adding behavior? Value-adding behaviors are what others have referred to as *critical few behaviors* (Daniels & Bailey, 2014) or *high-impact behaviors* (Braksick, 2004). Specifically, value-adding behaviors, whatever you call them, are the very behaviors that—when they happen, consistently performed by all the people who need to perform them at the right time—the individuals experience accomplishments, and the business sees the outcomes.

Imagine an assembly line where products are sent through a conveyor belt system and handled by more than one employee for multiple activities—inspection, tagging, sorting, packaging, and shipping, for example. The value-adding behaviors could be a select few per person. If everyone operates with a laser-sharp focus on those value-adding behaviors, the line runs smoothly, and packages are shipped precisely as they are supposed to be. Let us take another example, a therapist working with a family. The therapist is given a packet to gather information by the family, which is critical as the packet is submitted to the insurance funder for payment. The therapist's value-adding behavior is to capture the required information in the packet every time, without missing any item on the packet forms. One last example from the world of sports: in American football, players on the offense are organized on a line and have a very value-adding responsibility—keeping the defensive players away from the quarterback. Living up to this responsibility requires multiple value-adding behaviors, such as blocking and pushing and leg work for the linemen to position themselves like a human wall. What would happen if one of the linemen did not engage those value-adding behaviors? It's called a sack, and it's one of the most brutal hits in American football.

Value-adding behaviors are absolutely critical. There's no doubt that every position in every organization engages in many behaviors—some have suggested thousands to tens of thousands of behaviors a day if each and every one of them were counted. However, think back to those accomplishments. To achieve an accomplishment, and therefore yield a business outcome, one must engage in the "right" behaviors or, better said, those value-adding behaviors. But who determines which behaviors are of value?

Here's where good science comes in. If you want to know which behaviors are value-adding behaviors, you have two things to leverage: listening and seeing. Engaging with people who do the task, who know the task, and who train and coach others to do the task is critical to identify which behaviors are valuable to achieve accomplishments and outcomes. When working to identify value-added behaviors, start with asking people who do the work, train the work, and who were exemplars at completing the work. Once you have asked enough people for input, something emerges—trends of the most talked about behaviors. Chances are you identified those value-adding behaviors needed most. Do not stop there.

The second thing to use is sight. Directly observing the work in action is key. Scientists never assume anything; instead, they engage in the age-old tradition of direct observation of the phenomenon of interest. In the case of OBM, workplace settings are filled with opportunities to watch people do work, and if the problem being solved is that critical, then take the time to observe the work in action. Several questions will help you garner the very value-adding behaviors you are looking to define:

- What are people doing?
- What are they not doing that they should be, and why aren't they doing it?
- What is getting in their way?
- What is available to them within easy access to help them?
- What do we want them to do?
- Is anyone doing the desired behavior?
- Where are the exemplars, and what sets them apart from the others? Is what we want achievable?

As the heart of all this rhetoric, you should walk away with one notion about value-adding behaviors: if you want people to do a desired behavior, it needs to produce a desired accomplishment and outcome. Otherwise, it is not a value-adding behavior.

DEFINE BEHAVIOR

It should be of no surprise that business does not happen unless people behave. This premise is the very foundation of OBM, a study and supportive science to human behavior with the aim to maximize business outcomes.

In your own words, define behavior...

Write examples of behavior from your own workplace

Write examples of the major influences on behavior: learning history, organizational systems, accomplishments and outcomes.

DEFINE VALUE-ADDING BEHAVIOR

Value-adding behaviors are the critical few behaviors that matter at the end of everyday. What we do each day, the very behaviors we engage in, can be the difference between a productive day and a busy day.

How would you define value-adding behaviors?

Write examples of value-adding behaviors either those described in the course or your own. Note why they are "value-adding."

ACCOMPLISHMENTS FIRST, RESULTS SECOND

Photo by Sebastian Voortman from Pexels

We spoke a little bit about accomplishments already, but it's worth diving a bit deeper. To recap, accomplishments are what you experience from doing things (a sale, product launch, project completed). **Without a clear understanding of what people should accomplish from the work, you risk creating a situation where no one ever feels good about what they are doing. They fall into being busy versus being productive**. It's crucial for any supervisor, manager, or executive to have an eye on helping people experience those accomplishments. When working in customer service, one only has to look at the smile on a customer's face after helping them to feel a bit of accomplishment. The opposite is also important: in most cases, an unhappy customer doesn't lead to feeling accomplished. With a focus on accomplishments, you cannot set your sights on creating systems and the culture to be clear on what the accomplishments should be and to celebrate accomplishments when they are experienced.

As Carl Binder (2017) wrote in "What It Really Means to Be Accomplishment Based," "Unless accomplishments are tangible widgets, deliverables, or other physical products, we may not recognize them. Yet products of behavior such as decisions, relationships, ideas, strategies, and analyses are also accomplishments, but they are not always so easy to see" (p. 20).

Accomplishments can and should be countable. Binder (2017) wrote brilliantly about how, regardless of "whether the [accomplishment] is at the individual level (e.g., a budget that meets standards) or at the organizational level (e.g., a new market), or at any level in between, we want to focus on things that can be counted and evaluated as either meeting criteria for good or not" (p. 21). This countability leads to the carefully selected but useful understanding of business results, which are what follows accomplishments. Results are the outcomes following accomplishments (i.e., revenue from sales, customer satisfaction, better production yield). These results typically come from several accomplishments versus a one-to-one match. Without accomplishments along the way, results would simply not occur.

To motivate people, OBM teaches us to focus on accomplishments to encourage the "right" or value-adding behavior we want to see. When we write a job description or train a new hire, we tend to focus on the tasks they will be performing, and rightly so. Now imagine being focused while writing that job description or training that new hire on accomplishments—meaning you would inform the individual what they should experience when they demonstrate desirable behaviors. Right from the start, the individual is laser-focused on accomplishments versus just the task at hand. They know why it is important to both themselves and the organization. **Accomplishments become a differentiator to motivate people in the workplace, creating a focus of leaving work each day knowing they achieved something that benefited their employer.** Because you know accomplishments are tied to the end results or outcomes the business is seeking, you are now linking an individual's experience on the job with the bottom line of the organization. Other OBM practitioners have described this process as mapping behaviors to results. However, as we have already described, there is a missing piece between the two: accomplishments. The next time you write that job description, train that new hire, or even provide feedback and coaching to an employee, map it out for them:

What is the desirable value-adding behavior?

What accomplishment(s) should they experience?

What are the business outcomes we are striving to achieve?

Examples of Behaviors, Accomplishments, & Outcomes

Creating a budget à Budget meets standards à Below or at budget

Greeting a customer à Customer says thank you à Customer adds additional services

Packaging a product à Product meets specifications à Customer orders fulfilled

Working with an auditor à Auditor provides positive feedback à No Major Findings

Collaborating with a client à Client raves about your work à Customer Retention

Training a new employee à Employee meets requirements à Employee Retention

Providing Feedback à Positive Employee comments à Improve Performance

Driving Customer Orders à Deliver all orders on time à Positive Customer Satisfaction

Review Products in Inventory à Identified Sales Opportunities à Sold-Out Inventory

Learned new technology à Improved efficiency à Spend more time with customers

WHAT IS MEANT BY ACCOMPLISHMENTS AND AN ACCOMPLISHMENT BASED APPROACH?

Accomplishments are what we experience from doing things (e.g., making a sale, launching a product, completing a project).

As Carl Binder wrote in his 2017 article titled "What It Really Means to Be Accomplishment Based," "Unless accomplishments are tangible widgets, deliverables, or other physical products, we may not recognize them. Yet products of behavior such as decisions, relationships, ideas, strategies, and analyses are also accomplishments, but they are not always so easy to see."

Write examples of accomplishments from your own work experience

IDENTIFY BEHAVIOR, CONSEQUENCES, ACCOMPLISHMENTS, AND OUTCOMES/ BUSINESS RESULTS

See the example below. Then write your own set of examples

Behavior	Consequences	Accomplishments	Outcomes and Business Results
Filling out a client inquiry card	Client says they appreciate the customer service	Inquiry card resolved	Client complaints decrease

RESULTS, RESULTS, RESULTS

Photo by Lukas from Pexels

In the world of business, the higher in the organization you go, the more you will hear the word *results*. Why is that? Well, in brief, the higher you go, the more your behavior is influenced by the ultimate final outcome the organization desires, namely results. Sales, profits, safety, market share, customer satisfaction, growth, and scaling are all examples of what the focus is for executives of both small and large organizations. Without these results, organizations simply don't sustain. For the OBM practitioner, this lesson is important to remember—your work must be anchored and aimed toward achieving some business result. All the behavior change in the world doesn't mean anything if the bottom line is not impacted. This premise is the very essence for focusing on critical or high-impact behaviors, as we previously mentioned—and what it takes to achieve those outcomes are observable behaviors.

"OBM's mission is to improve performance in organizations" (Hyten, 2009, p. 92). It is simply this notion that drives the OBM practitioner. A definition of performance serves us all well, and Hyten (2009) illustrated a common definition used in OBM: **performance = behavior + results (p. 92)**.

Why Behaviors and Results?

- Every job has specific behaviors and results associated with it.
- When you pinpoint behaviors only, you may not achieve the desired results.
- When you pinpoint results only, you may inadvertently reinforce the wrong behaviors.

Daniels and Bailey (2014) provided some great direction on differentiating behavior and results.

> **Behavior** is what people are doing, while **Results** are what people have produced.

> **Behavior** is what you see people do when they are working, while **Results** are what you see after people stop working.

> **Behavior** required direct observation of what people are doing, while **Results** does not require seeing people do anything.

> **Behavior** typically is written or spoken in the present tense with verbs ending in "ing," while **Results** are in the past tense.

> **Behavior** is expressed with words preceding the behavior such as "by, through, and to," while **Results** are expressed with phrases such as "in order to..., so that..., and to achieve..."

The following are Examples of Behaviors and Results from several OBM projects over the years. Each one is associated with either a strategic effort to improve safety within an organization, or a strategic imperative within a Human Resources department.

BEHAVIORS	RESULTS
Lifting with knees when carrying items greater than 25 lbs.	Reduction in injuries related to improper lifting
Wearing Fall Protection when working at elevated heights	Reduction in injuries related to falls from heights
Completing Safe Work Permits	Safety protocols designs for non-routine tasks and high hazard tasks
Completing Job Safety Analyses	Hazards identified and mitigated
Identifying Safety Action Items	Improved safe work conditions and systems implemented by management and cross functional teams
Modifying onboarding process flow with cross functional team	Business Operations
Communicating monthly updates on HR policies and procedures	Compliance with policies and procedures
Conducting quarterly employee satisfaction surveys	Employee Retention
Supporting employees regarding benefits	Benefits enrollment, Costs
Facilitating leadership training programs	Employee Retention, Promotions

The Link Between Behaviors and Results

Gravina et al. (2017) provided readers with an illustrative model to show the connection between Behaviors and Results. Commonly used by OBM practitioners, this model gives clients a clear idea of who does what and to what result. Facilitating the discussion with clients and colleagues to create such an illustration requires time, data, and patience. Following a series of meetings, individual and group interviews, and computer time, the output is a map, what some have called a Behavior Map, or Behavior-Results Map, or Alignment Map.

Whatever you decide to call it, the focus is on identifying the critical behaviors each major role demonstrates to support achieving the business results. Below examples from work conducted by OBM practitioners – safety examples and examples related to a strategic imperative within a Human Resources department.

EXECUTIVE BEHAVIORS	MANAGEMENT TEAM BEHAVIORS	SUPERVISOR BEHAVIORS	EMPLOYEE BEHAVIORS	RESULTS
Set vision and direction Recognition of improvements Approve budget, and resources	Participate in BBS Steering Teams Provide direction based on data trends and improvement needs Recognition of improvements	Conduct BBS observations weekly Participate in BBS Steering Teams Provide feedback on data trends and improvement needs	Conduct BBS observations weekly Participate in BBS Steering Teams	80% participation in Behavior Based Safety Execution Reduction in injuries and incidents
Set vision and direction Recognition of improvements Set organizational needs and priorities for employee professional development	Take action on satisfaction survey results Monitoring performance review completion Allocate resources and budget for professional development	Encourage participation on satisfaction surveys Facilitate performance reviews Allocate time for professional development activities	Provide feedback on employee satisfaction surveys Complete actions from performance reviews Complete professional development activities	Retention Promotions Professional Development Plans improving

Behavior Is All About Context

When it comes to identifying behaviors, the OBM practitioner takes careful consideration to ensure the pinpoints are value-adding behaviors. Value-adding behaviors can simply be defined as the pinpoints that make a major difference towards achieving the desired outcomes. In the consulting practice, it was common to facilitating the discussion with clients on identifying value-adding behaviors by asking one question – "if everyone, and we mean everyone, did one behavior that had the highest probability of achieving the outcome, what would that one behavior be?"

At this point, a list of pinpoints would have been identified beforehand, and the business outcomes would have been listed as well.

Below are examples from work conducted by OBM practitioners – safety examples and examples related to a strategic imperative within a Human Resources department.

BEHAVIORS	VALUE-ADDING BEHAVIORS
Lifting with knees when carrying items greater than 25 lbs.	Employees take 15 minutes breaks after 25 minutes of continuous work of lifting with knees when carrying items greater than 25 lbs.
Wearing Fall Protection when working at elevated heights	Employee's test and confirm with spotter use of fall protection equipment prior to working at elevated heights
Completing Safe Work Permits	Employees work in teams prior to starting work requiring Safe Work Permits per the company's requirements
Completing Job Safety Analyses	Employees work in teams to identify and mitigate hazards following detailed steps of the task using the approved Job Safety Analyses form
Identifying Safety Action Items	Management team members facilitate discussions with employees on identifying Safety Action Items to improve safety, documented in Safety Action Item log, and reviewed monthly with employees.
Modify onboarding process flow with cross functional team	HR Director facilitates cross functional team to document process flow and actions to improve onboarding process
Communicating monthly updates on HR policies and procedures	HR communications team writes monthly updates for the employee newsletter regarding HR policies and procedures with follow-up activity plan to discuss with employees during team meetings.
Conducting quarterly employee satisfaction surveys	HR team works with business unit managers on employee satisfaction surveys to ensure employees receive, complete, and get results following completion.
Supporting employees regarding benefits	HR team works one-on-one with employees to enroll employees in desired benefits available by the organization and troubleshoot any issues.
Facilitating leadership training programs	HR Director and team members design, facilitate and follow up on leadership development training programs with high potential leaders

Value-Adding Behaviors to Accomplishments to Business Outcomes

Photo by fauxels from Pexels

Let's put it all together. We have discussed value adding behavior, accomplishments, and business outcomes. As an OBM practitioner, you can bring it all together for your customers by mapping it out.

Below are examples from work conducted by OBM practitioners – safety examples and examples related to a strategic imperative within a Human Resources department.

What is the desirable value adding behaviors?	What accomplishment(s) should they experience?	What are the business outcomes we are striving to achieve?
1. Employees take 15 minutes breaks after 25 minutes of continuous work of lifting with knees when carrying items greater than 25 lbs.	1. Tasks completed and avoided feeling of fatigue.	1. Reduction in injuries related to improper lifting.
2. Employee's test and confirm with spotter use of fall protection equipment prior to working at elevated heights	2. Tasks completed without incident or injury.	2. Reduction in injuries related to falls from heights.
3. Employees work in teams prior to starting work requiring Safe Work Permits per the companies' requirements.	3. Tasks completed as a team and positive feedback from supervisors/ managers regarding safe work permit.	3. Safety protocols designs for non-routine tasks and high hazard tasks.
4. Employees work in teams to identify and mitigate hazards following detailed steps of the task using the approved Job Safety Analyses (JSA) form	4. Tasks completed, hazards eliminated protecting employees and positive feedback from supervisors/managers regarding JSA.	4. Hazards identified and mitigated.
5. HR Director facilitates cross functional team to document process flow and actions to improve onboarding process.	5. Process Improvement efforts identified and implemented.	5. Business Operations.
6. HR communications team writes monthly updates for the employee newsletter	6. Employees give positive feedback on updates and discussions.	6. Compliance with policies and procedures

regarding HR policies and procedures with follow-up activity plan to discuss with employees during team meetings.		
7. HR team works with business unit managers on employee satisfaction surveys to ensure employees receive, complete, and get results following completion.	7. Survey response rate, positive feedback from employees, actionable steps to improve.	7. Employee Retention
8. HR team works one-on-one with employees to enroll employees in desired benefits available by the organization and troubleshoot any issues.	8. Employees questions are answered, enrollment in benefits.	8. Cost

The Bottom Line and Beyond

Photo by Philipp Birmes from Pexels

We've already highlighted behaviors, accomplishments, and outcomes, and for this section, we wanted to ensure you get a deeper look at the types of results the OBM practitioner should be aiming to achieve. Your goal isn't just bottom-line business results.

Bottom-line results

First, bottom-line business results. Depending on the industry, business model, and customers, the business is aiming for some outcome, result, bottom-line business that defines the business purpose. Here are some examples:

- Telecommunications business: To supply customers with what is needed to meet their communication needs.
- Banking business: To provide the means for customers to access their money and provide services and products for various money matters.
- Human services business: To provide quality and ethically sound services to their clientele.

MANUEL "MANNY" RODRIGUEZ, DBA, BCBA

Such results are simply what differentiates a company from the competition from the perspective of ultimate performance.

Effective change execution

Second, effectiveness of change execution. Behavior changes to achieve business results is clearly the focus as an outcome. To achieve the outcome, you must effectively execute a strategy. During the implementation of an OBM strategy, the OBM practitioner spends a great deal of time analyzing "how" the strategy is being implemented. There are quite a few techniques OBM practitioners utilize to ensure execution effectiveness.

Leadership effectiveness

Third, leadership effectiveness. OBM strategies are implemented with a great deal of work on the part of the leaders who comprise the organization. From the front line to the executive board room, leaders are part of the implementation of any behavior to get results in any change effort. OBM practitioners absolutely focus on the end results of leadership effectiveness—were the results achieved the right way from the standpoint of leaders being great leaders? The goal is to achieve a "yes" to this question. But what leadership behaviors make a difference when implementing change strategies? Fortunately, a great deal of research and literature exists in the field of OBM to help focus on such leadership skills and behaviors.

Organizational culture

Fourth, organizational culture. "The way we do things around here" is a common definition of culture. When engaging in change efforts, in fact, a result is changing the organizational culture. Imagine trying to make a change to a procedure without changing the culture. Once the project team declares victory, the culture will reinforce people going back to the way things were before. In other words, the culture will reign supreme if the change does not actually change the culture. How do you effect change from an organizational culture standpoint?

According to behavior science, a great deal of culture change begins with values, performance management, and leadership.

Categories of business results most common in organizations

Revenue, sales, productivity, quality, and safety are the most common categories of business results.

Write examples of business results you are familiar with. Be as specific as possible.

REFLECT ON A PAST STRATEGIC INITIATIVE, AND IDENTIFY THE RESULTS USING THE FOUR CATEGORIES BELOW—WHAT WERE THE RELEVANT FOCUS AREAS, METRICS, AND MEASURES OF SUCCESS

Bottom-line business results

Effective change execution

Leadership effectiveness

Organizational culture

BRINGING SCIENCE
TO MANAGEMENT

Photo by fauxels from Pexels

W hat comes to mind when you think of a scientist? As a child, you probably related scientists with lab coats, Bunsen burners, and beakers. As an adult, you may think of a university professor, biologists, chemist, or physicist perhaps. Originally published in 1911, Frederick Winslow Taylor introduced the world to his principles of scientific management, which is the focus of this section.

Taylor's Four Principles

1. Replace the "rule of thumb." Management should be focused on using science for a person's work.
2. Training and developing a person to work are based on a scientific approach instead of a "as best as I can" model.
3. Collaboration is paramount to success, ensuring the work being done is scientific in nature—defining the problem to solve, measuring the work, sticking to, and evaluating the plan, and so on.
4. The work and responsibilities are equally divided between management and employees.

More than a hundred years later, these principles still hold true. Applying a scientific approach to human performance in the workplace not only differentiates a successful manager from failed ones but also differentiates between growing and profitable companies from those that close their doors. The ever-growing science of OBM offers additional principles for practitioners to plan a scientific approach to the management of human performance. These principles, or what the original authors called *dimensions of behavior* (Baer et al., 1968), support a scientific approach to identifying, understanding, and supporting behavior improvement in various applications.

The Seven Dimensions of OBM

Photo by Jakub Novacek from Pexels

1. **Applied:** The behavior, accomplishments, and outcomes of interest are targeted problems worth solving. The applied means it is a matter of interest to stakeholders and society versus theory or someone's pet project.

2. **Behavioral:** Behavior is the focus, but OBM practitioners also focus on the relationship between behavior and its relationship to accomplishments and the business outcomes.

   a. ***Note:** At this point, it may seem like the information in this work is redundant but consider the repetition as being important to your OBM knowledge and know-how since behavior is one of the main differentiators of what makes OBM so unique.

2. **Analytic:** Scientists analyze, OBM practitioners are scientists, and OBM practitioners approach management as scientists. Being analytical requires looking at data, evaluating the data, and hearing what story the data is telling you. If you are not looking at data and taking time to analyze it, you may in fact be employing a game of luck—which is not at all advisable in the world of business.

3. **Technological**: This principle is all about your technique of execution. Imagine that you wanted to replicate someone else's work because the results were so good. When you go to do so, you find holes in their work, so you must interpret what they did and how they did it. As a result, your outcomes are not favorable. In fact, they may be totally opposite of what you expected. The technological principle aims to avoid that and is all about writing what you do, how you do it, and what the outcomes were, specifically with the intention that it can be replicated. If you are a manager or executive with multiple business units, teams, or divisions, and something works in one, you more than likely would like it to be implemented in the others. By following technologically sound methods, you are more likely to have equal or even greater success when replicating.

4. **Conceptually systematic:** Scientists rely on historically proven science and theory to guide everything they do. Makes sense, right? As a manager, you should (mostly) do the same: take the guess work out of the equation, and don't rely solely on your personal experience or that of others. Before you implement a solution to solve a problem, you should ideally prove that the solution is grounded on past science, meaning someone else proved it

before you. At the very least, a theory should guide what you are looking to do.

5. **Effective:** It worked! That is the gist of effective. This principle is intended to guide practitioners to the point of everything they are trying to do—solve problems that matter. OBM practitioners look to ensure the change happens as planned and is in fact significant to stakeholders.

6. **Generality:** This principle is like the technological dimension in that OBM practitioners are looking to replicate successes. If you cannot replicate successes, what is the point, really? For organizations, best practices are typically shared across the corporation. If a merger and acquisition is successful, the executive team would look to replicate it, assuming several variables are similar. For a manager, a success story becomes a building block for promotions and professional growth—replicating successes is even more so. By focusing your work to ensure generality, you are building a portfolio of success stories, ones that are also replicable by others.

The Scientific Method

Photo by fauxels from Pexels

It is worth a few moments of reading to revisit something many have learned in primary education: the scientific method. To be a scientist manager—whether you're an OBM practitioner, a supervisor in a manufacturing setting, a manager in a human service organization, or an executive of a financial institution—applying the scientific method will ensure you're following the seven dimensions of OBM described above and doing so with Taylor's principles of scientific management.

The scientific method is typically written in the following sequential steps to keep the scientist organized and to maintain integrity of the scientific process:

Step 1. Define the problem to solve. Typically, in the form of a question to answer or based on observation, managers would formulate a problem to solve. In either case, defining what problem to solve for is critical to proceed.

Step 2. Create a hypothesis. Why do you think the problem is happening? Having a hypothesis becomes the foundation of how to best approach the problem. Depending on your hypothesis, you may have some ideas on who to seek input from or what to observe for, but you may also have no clue and need to investigate. That means you are guessing as your hypothesis, but at this point, that's okay. Science comes into play in the next steps.

Step 3. Research the problem. Do not guess at the solution. Others may have faced the same problem, so a little research in practice can go a long way. What have others experienced with the same or even similar problems? How did they approach the problems? What were the results? What would they do differently next time?

Step 4. Gather data and measure the problem. Data, data, data. Did we say data? Okay, you get the idea: science requires data collection. What is the size of the problem? How long has it existed? What has been previously tried to solve it? Getting data and then continuing with ongoing tracking of the data is the scientific way. In management, data is crucial to problem-solving, performance management, and overall showing success or failure when it happens.

Step 5. Analyze the problem and decide on solutions. Based on Steps 3 and 4, you are gathering the information you need to analyze the problem and determine viable (hopefully previously proven) solutions. With a proper analysis, you will be able to identify solutions to experiment with (see Step 6), and get the problem solved. Without analysis, you may be still guessing.

Step 6. Experiment. In the world of business, the experiment step is called *pilot testing*. In some cases, such testing is not practical, but in most cases, pilot testing will arguably save you time, money, and stress if you pilot tests your solutions toward problem-solving. In addition, pilot testing gives you the opportunity to learn from your stakeholders (i.e., the employees you are asking to do things differently at work or are asking more of). By experimenting, you are taking a scientific approach to your management practice, not guessing. Thus, testing, trying solutions, and getting feedback are all critical steps in the process. Feedback will occur in two parts during experimentation: (a) the data you are collecting and (b) when people will tell you what they think, which also data but more of a validation of what people think and feel about the solution versus the hard numbers. This step is critical to resolving the problem.

Step 7. Go big or go back. This step is not written like a scientist, but the premise here is that, after experimenting, you will analyze the results and determine whether to go big, meaning full-scale implementation across the organization or beyond the pilot anyway, or go back, meaning back to the drawing board (Steps 1–6).

Step 8. Conclude, and keep moving. You will draw conclusions from your work thus far. Was it effective? Can it generalize to other business units, divisions, etc.? Did you achieve what you set out to achieve (see Step 1)? Reach your conclusions and decide whether to keep moving or claim victory. In the world of work, you will more than likely choose to keep moving.

Just like a scientist, management, and practitioners of OBM alike make good use of the power of direct observation. Having your eyes and ears focused on the value-adding behaviors, the accomplishments, and the outcomes is a key differentiator of OBM. When starting your OBM path, one of the best things to do is simply observe work in action. Taking time to observe, with your own eyes, people working hard to produce something gives you great insight into what is really happening. Listening to your stakeholders who are looking for performance improvement is equally critical to the experiment of the solution itself. They provide the keys to making things happen. More than likely, they're living with the problem and working around it, or are just frustrated that it hasn't yet been solved. At worst, they are complacent to problem, saying things like "it is what it is, we just deal with it." A scientist would want to solve the problem. A manager would want to solve the problem. Hence, the manager is a scientist, and OBM is the perfect science for a manager.

To employ a scientific approach, OBM practitioners heavily utilize the power of asking really good questions to get stakeholders involved in the process. Accordingly, interviewing skills have greatly supported practitioners of OBM, and whether you are an external consultant, internal change agent, or supervisor/manager/executive of a company, interviewing skills will be a great asset to you in using science and making things happen.

Irving Seidman (2013) argued that interviewing techniques and skills are a comprehensive yet digestible way for researchers to collect data—a process that is applicable to OBM practitioners and management alike. Here, we simply summarize Seidman's 13 techniques and encourage managers and OBM practitioners to hone their interviewing skills. Doing so will help maximize their scientific work in improving performance.

1. **Listen more:** Listen to what the interviewee is saying, and search for the "inner voice," meaning what struggles the interviewee is facing versus the surface level they would share publicly. While listening, pay attention to time and the process of the interview, which requires less talking and more listening and attending to what's happening.

2. **Follow up**: Ask for clarification, go deeper into the context and situation, and explore appropriately with the interviewee.

3. **Ask real questions:** Ask questions to which you don't already know or could anticipate the responses and use open-ended versus leading questions.

4. **Follow up but do not interrupt:** As the point states, do not interrupt. When interviewing, take note of any points the interviewee discusses, and then follow up on each point.

5. **Try one of these approaches**: (a) Have the interviewee talk to you as if you were someone else, someone the interviewee would be more comfortable talking to. (b) Have the interview tell a story that describes what would be more conceptual or vague; stories are more specific.

6. **Ask interviewee to reconstruct and for details**: Reconstructing situations and context is better than relying on the interviewee's memory. Reconstructing allows for the interviewee to focus on what is now important.

7. **Keep interviewees focused**: Ensure you create a structure and focus for the interview. Guide the conversation toward maintaining the focus of the interview.

8. **Accept that ebbs and flows happen**: From one interview to the next with the same interviewee, expect it to not flow gradually or seamlessly. Do not take it personally. Instead, work with the structure, and guide the conversation.

9. **Limit your interaction**: As the interviewer, you should occasionally reciprocate experiences the interviewee describes to be personable, but not each and every point. In addition, avoid reinforcing the participant's responses as it can distract from the structure, time, and focus of the interview.

10. **Explore laughter**: When an interviewee laughs, it may be because they said something funny, but it may also mean they are nervous or are struggling with a point. Exploring the laugh may prove to be valuable for more context or reconstruction of the story.

11. **Hunches are okay to follow**: During the interview process, you're observing verbal and non-verbal behavior. If you observe behavior that contradicts the responses by the interviewee (e.g., mannerisms, poor eye contact, etc.), you could ask about your observations to further explore whether your hunch was right or wrong.

12. **Use a guide but be cautious**: Interview guides can be very helpful to maintain focus and structure. However, the questions on the guide may be of little interest to the interviewee. You should therefore use the guide but be flexible so that you can work with the interviewee's responses.

13. **Tolerate silence:** Be patient if the interviewee is taking time to respond. Silence for seconds may see like a long time, but that time can provide a great deal of information.

Common OBM Diagnostic Tools

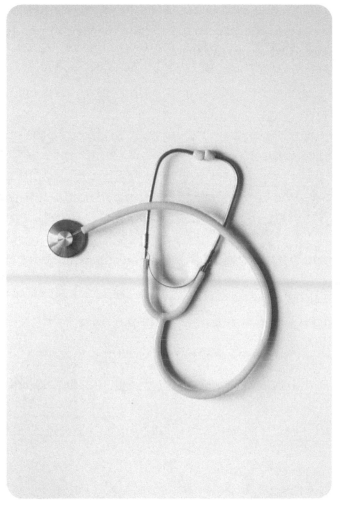

Photo by Karolina Grabowska from Pexels

ABC analysis

The ABC analysis is a special tool for the OBM practitioner to formulate the intricate link between a given behavior, the antecedents (A) that came before the behavior (B), and the consequences (C) that followed the behavior (i.e., antecedent => behavior => consequence). Known as the *three-term contingency*, this model supports documenting the real situation happening and determining whether the desired behavior has adequate antecedents and consequences.

Using ABC as a problem-solving process, the OBM practitioner looks to determine which antecedents and consequences currently influence the desired and undesired behaviors. Both types of behaviors are ultimately listed and analyzed.

The ABC analysis helps you discover patterns among A's and C's. Are the antecedents always present before the behavior occurs? Are they impactful enough to trigger the behavior each and every time?

Consequences have at least four important dimensions to be analyzed:

1. **Impact:** Does the consequence increase or decrease the behavior from happening in the future?

2. **Timeliness:** Was the consequence experienced immediately after the behavior occurred or after a delay in time?

3. **Likelihood:** What is the probability the consequence is experienced by the individual?

4. **Importance:** What is the relative importance of the consequence to the individual?

   a. The strongest consequences are high impact, immediate, likely, and important.
   b. Most behaviors that don't happen are low impact, delayed, unlikely, and unimportant.

There are typically six steps to conducting an ABC analysis:

1. Define the problem behavior
2. Define the desired performance
3. Identify the severity of the problem—is it worth the time and effort to solve?
4. Conduct the ABC analysis for the problem behavior
5. Conduct the ABC analysis for desired performance (remember, value-adding behavior)
6. Evaluate whether the A's and C's for the desired behavior will actually work

Below are examples from work conducted by OBM practitioners – safety examples and examples related to a strategic imperative within a Human Resources department.

Antecedent	Behavior	Consequences
New Employee Employee request Renewal Period	Reviewing and enrolling employees in benefits package	Employee enrollment Positive feedback from employee
Risk of falling - Working at Heights. Safe Work permit. Regulatory requirements.	Wearing a harness to climb above 6 feet to rooftop.	Secured on roof top. Positive feedback from Supervisor.

PDC

Dr. John Austin (2000) created the PDC, one of the most heavily researched tools in OBM today. The PDC is an interview-based assessment that covers **four** areas that contribute to performance problems: (a) antecedents and information, (b) equipment and processes, (c) knowledge and skills, and (d) consequences.

Generally, the PDC is used as an interviewing tool by the OBM practitioner, delivered to managers and employees alike, but specifically to subject matter experts (SMEs) who can speak to the performance problem.

In large organizations or businesses with multiple sites, the PDC can be delivered using a sampling approach. The PDC can and should also be used in conjunction with direct observation methods, such as ABC analysis.

Let's review each of the four areas regarding the questions asked within the PDC.

Antecedents and information

- Is there a written job description telling exactly what is expected of the employee?
- Has the employee received adequate instruction about what to do?
- Are employees aware of the mission of the department/organization? Can they tell you what it is?

- Are there job or task aids in the employees' immediate environment? Are the aids visible while employees are completing the task in question? Are there reminders to prompt the task at the correct time?
- Is the supervisor present during task completion?
- Are there frequently updated, challenging, and attainable goals set that employees are comfortable with/feel are fair?

Knowledge and skills

- Can the employee tell you what they are supposed to be doing and how to do it?
- Have the performers received any training before starting work?
- Do the performers understand the consequence of both good and poor performance?
- Do the performers understand the concepts needed to perform well?
- Do the performers have sufficient basic skills—reading and so on?
- Can the employees physically demonstrate the completion of the task?
- Do the employee have the capacity to complete the job?

Equipment and process

- Is task completion dependent on unreliable equipment?
- Are the equipment and environment optimally arranged in a physical sense?
- Are larger processes suffering from certain incomplete tasks along the way (process disconnects)?
- Are these processes logically arranged, without unnecessary repetition?
- Are there any other obstacles keeping employees from completing the task?

Consequences

- Are there consequences delivered contingent on the task?
  - Frequency?
  - Immediacy?
  - Consistency/probability?
  - Positive or negative?
  - Are there Premack* reinforcers?
- Do employees see the effects of performance?
- Do supervisors deliver feedback?
- Is there performance monitoring?
- Is there a response effort associated with performing?

- Are there other behaviors competing with the desired performance?

*Premack reinforcers are consequences delivered as a condition of demonstrating a specific behavior or set of behaviors. Typically, described as a "if you do this behavior, you will receive this consequence."

5 steps to using the PDC

In practice, the PDC can be conceptualized and used in a 5-step process:

1. Identify the problem to improve.
2. Define the desired target behavior and key stakeholders (leaders, performers, subject matter experts).
3. Determine potential for improvement, and link to bottom-line results (revenue, customer satisfaction, etc.).
4. Conduct interviews using the PDC: informant-based assessments.
5. Report conclusions and provide research-based solutions.

After interviewing SMEs, and hopefully more than a few individuals would be interviewed, you will compile the information for evaluation. In the literature, the PDC includes yes and no responses to support the analysis of the data in aggregate. However, a simple number of yeses and noes can be deceiving. The OBM practitioner takes extra time to evaluate each question in detail to ensure the "right" things are in place to enable performance.

Below are examples from work conducted by OBM practitioners – safety examples and examples related to a strategic imperative within a Human Resources department.

The PDC: Safety Example — Employees Removing Pallets

Antecedents and Information	Equipment and Processes	Knowledge and Skills	Consequences
• No job aide or instructions – viewed as "easy work." • Infrequent task • Relates to safety, value and mission of company is "safety first", some risk in pallet removal (sharp edges, lifting)	• Pallet removal is manual versus using some machinery like a forklift or dolly cart. • Forklifts are dedicated to production/distribution work.	• Employees remove pallets differently, no standard way. • Some use gloves and safety glasses, others do not • All employees recognize proper lifting, waste location, and have demonstrated such behaviors.	• Removing pallets is an assigned task, given infrequently to employees. • Removed pallets results in organized workspaces, positive effect of performance • Supervisors do not provide feedback, viewed as "easy." • Production and maintenance work takes priorities over pallet removal as they have goals and rewards associated with them.

The PDC: HR Example — Supervisors following the disciplinary process

Antecedents and Information	Equipment and Processes	Knowledge and Skills	Consequences
• Little to no instructions given to supervisors • No job aide on the process • No goals but not relevant for this process, only used as-needed and deemed appropriate	• No significant issues identified	• Supervisors can describe the process at a high level. Details are fuzzy for most supervisors • Not a lot of experience for most supervisors	• Infrequently used process • Inconsistently applied across supervisors • Many supervisors avoid disciplinary processes • Supervisors prefer

Process mapping

A great deal of literature focuses on process mapping and process improvement. One of the main sources on the subject comes from the great work of Rummler and Brache (1995). Their book, *Improving Performance: How to Manage the White Space on the Organization Chart,* now in its third edition, is undoubtably one of the main required reads for the OBM practitioner. For the purposes of our book, we will cover the following:

- SIPOC model
- Three levels of performance
- Seven deadly sins of process improvement
- Nine variables of performance
- Process mapping 101 (how to)

SIPOC model

SIPOC stands for supplier, inputs, work process, outputs, and customers. The model provides the practitioner and the key stakeholders a big-picture view of the ins and outs of a given process. Whether related to production, distribution, customer service, or sales, each work process has specific inputs provided by suppliers and identified outputs for the given customer. Within this high-level model are requirements and feedback loops. These loops are central to the model as they provide great information for how the overall structure is operating, or not operating. In practice, the SIPOC model is facilitated by the OBM practitioner to work with the stakeholders to "map out" the SIPOC elements for a given process. Before you get deeply into a specific work process, map out the big picture; doing so may in fact help everyone see what goes into and comes out of the process and whether everyone sees it the same way or differently.

Below are examples from work conducted by OBM practitioners – safety examples and examples related to a strategic imperative within a Human Resources department.

S.I.P.O.C. Example Human Resources Onboarding Process

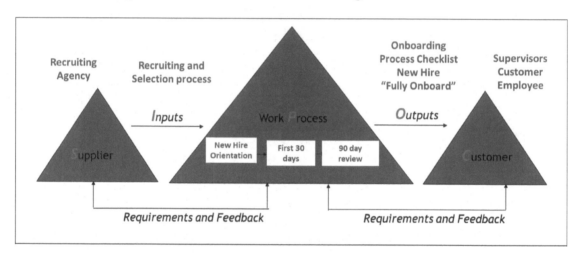

S.I.P.O.C. Example Safety Hazard Communication

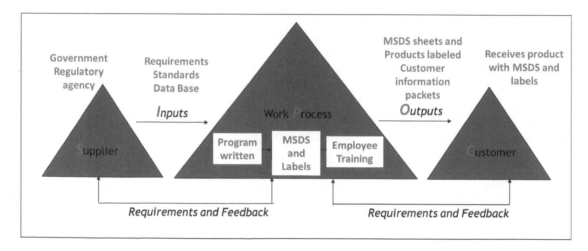

Three levels of performance

Rummler and Brache (1995) provided a clear understanding of the three levels of performance to analyze: organizational level, process level, and job/performer level.

The organizational level is where strategy is established. This level of analysis guides the OBM practitioner to analyze the situation from the customer viewpoint, the supplier viewpoint, the employee viewpoint, and the shareholder viewpoint. The focus of this level is to understand how the organization operations function as a processing system—the inputs and outputs. The goal is to learn as much as possible during an analysis of the organizational level; all organizations should be nimble to continuously adapt to change.

There are three shortcomings of not managing the organizational level:

- Various quality efforts are not driven by a clearly stated organizational strategy.
- The organization has not been designed in a way that supports maximum quality.
- The organization is not managed with quality as the driver.

The process level is where workflows are streamlined. Processes, of course, are the series of steps designed to produce a product or service. There are three types of processes to evaluate:

1. **Primary processes:** The outputs for to the customer.
2. **Support processes:** The supporting management of the business, such as recruiting, training, and purchasing.
3. **Management processes:** The actions managers take to support the business, such as strategic planning and performance management.

There are two shortcomings of not managing the process level: (a) silos are created or reinforced, and (b) disconnects form between the organization and individual employees.

The job/performer level requires the OBM practitioner to look at jobs at all levels and at the performers who serve in those jobs.

When analyzing the job/performer level, many actions are seen to be influencing performance improvement—train them, transfer them, coach, and counsel them, discipline them, and replace them. **The "them" are employees, and they are not broken**. What *is* analyzed at the job performer level are the inputs, performer expectations, outputs, consequences, and feedback loops to the performer. These are intricate and require time and effort from all parties to truly get a great picture of the work happening at the job/performer level. The outcome of this level of analysis is a detailed view of the work on the ground floor.

There are two shortcomings of not managing the job/performer level: (a) organizational and process improvements will not happen if they, the employees, are not part of the job, and (b) the environment of the job ultimately needs to support the performer.

To summarize the three levels of analysis, the OBM practitioner looks at the organization with a holistic view. Each level has many intricacies. The organizational level focuses on strategy, structure, policy, and measurement systems; the process level focuses on the workflow; and the job/performer level focuses on the skills, knowledge, ability, and rewards each individual experiences. The big picture shows the suppliers and customers linking it all together.

Seven deadly sins of process improvement

By identifying the seven deadly sins of process improvement, Rummler and Brache (1995) provided practitioners and managers with some helpful guidance on things to avoid. Each of the seven deadly sins of process improvement demonstrate real potential challenges organizations face when looking to improve processes and, ultimately, performance. Let us review each of the seven deadly sins and some tips on managing through them.

Sin 1. Process improvement not tied to the strategic issues the business faces. Process improvement should be driven by an issue critical to the organization, such as profitability, market share, regulatory compliance, safety, or customer satisfaction. Process improvement should be tied to measurable goals—improving by 35%, reducing errors, cutting costs, and decreasing time to complete process. These critical business issues typically require cross-functional processes; thus, the impact is major, and a holistic view of performance is essential. Finally, top management support is required for process improvement as they are the decision-makers and key stakeholders of strategic issues.

Sin 2. The process improvement effort does not involve the right people, especially top management, in the right way. Process improvement should not be done by outsiders (consultants) but rather by the very people involved in the process. Consultants serve a purpose in process improvement, such as facilitating and providing guidance on the methods of process improvement, but the authorship of the processes themselves belongs to the doers. The right people can include customers and suppliers as well, and in some cases, they should be included. The process improvement effort should also include a sponsor or owner of the process; such individuals are the right people at the top management level to hold people accountable and are ultimately responsible for the results. Lastly, the right people are a steering team, which is a cross-functional group in charge of the process improvement effort.

Sin 3. Process improvement teams are not given a clear, appropriate charter and are not held accountable for fulfilling that charter. A project charter enables the team in many ways. First, a clear sense of assignments (roles), direction, and boundaries are established. The driving issue and the "why" has been selected and defined—something clearly driven by top management. The specific goals are written and detailed. Roles and responsibilities are clearly delineated. Deliverables are clearly identified. If there are any constraints, or "off limits" areas of the business, those are also identified in a charter. Deadlines, timelines, and schedules of work are documented in the charter. In addition, what happens to the team members' "regular jobs" while they are involved in the project is defined. Finally, how the team will be rewarded for their contributions may be defined as well, and we would encourage this aspect be included.

Sin 4. The top management team thinks that, if it's not "nuking" the existing organization ("reengineering"), it's not making significant improvements. Reengineering a process does not require reorganization, restructuring, or reduction. Measure success in terms of the degree to which you have solved the problem. In most cases, process improvements may be seen as subtle, minor, or "small" changes. However, what we have learned through process improvement efforts for years now is that, sometimes, small changes make a big impact. Focus on the impact.

Sin 5. Process designers don't sufficiently consider how the changes will affect the people who have to work in the new process. Process improvement is not a "field of dreams" approach. Have the people who have to work in the new process involved from the beginning of the improvement effort. These individuals provide a sanity check. An old saying exists (not sure who said it first, unfortunately) that applies here: authorship = ownership. The process should be doable by the very people being asked to do the work. By considering who is affected by the change, it's clear how their jobs will change, how their measures/goals will change, and what exactly is entailed in the change.

Sin 6. The organization focuses more on redesign than on implementation. Process redesign is an entirely academic endeavor until implementation. For a complex process, implementation often lasts nine to 18 months as a general rule of thumb. Why so long? Process improvement across departments or business units is a change in how people perform work, and change requires careful attention to people, process, and outcomes. Implementation requires equipping the organization to absorb the change, appointing an implementation leader, and establishing detailed action plans, defining roles and rewards as quick examples. The group is often six to 10 times more people than were involved in the design process. In short, the work on implementation is about managing effort, which is required to be much more significant when implementing the process than when redesigning the process.

Sin 7. Teams fail to leave behind a measurement system and other parts of the infrastructure necessary for continuous process improvement. From process improvement (project) to process management (continuous improvement), continuous improvement is the maintenance part of process improvement. "Process Management must rest on a foundation of measures" …[and] "management must monitor performance" (RummlerBrache, 2020, p. 8). Senior level owners of key processes are also in place. Process management ultimately ensures the focus on this process is maintained.

Nine variables of performance

Before learning how to do process mapping as part of process improvement, the OBM practitioner must understand the nine variables of performance, as described by Rummler and Brache (1995).

We start back at the three levels of performance. Each level of performance includes three performance variables: goals, design, and management performance variables. These components add up to what they refer to as the nine performance variables (three levels of performance, each with three variables).

At the organizational level, the following model highlights the relevant goals, design, and management performance variables:

- Goals performance variables:
    a. Has the strategy/direction been articulated and communicated?

    b. Does the strategy make sense in terms of external and internal threats, opportunities, strengths, and weaknesses?
    c. Have the required outputs and the level of performance expected been determined and communicated?

- Design performance variables:
  - a. Are all relevant functions in place?
  - b. Are all functions necessary?
  - c. Is the current flow of inputs and outputs between functions appropriate?
  - d. Does the formal organization structure support the strategy?

- Management performance variables:
  - a. Have the appropriate functional goals been set?
  - b. Is relevant performance measured?
  - c. Are resources appropriately allocated?
  - d. Are the interfaces between functions being managed?

At the process level, the following model highlights the relevant goals, design, and management performance variables:

1. Goals performance variable:
   a. Are goals for key processes linked to customer and organizational requirements?

2. Design performance variables:
   a. Does a process (*IS map* versus *should map*) exist?
   b. Is this the most efficient and effective process for accomplishing the goals?

3. Management performance variables:
   a. Have appropriate process sub-goals been set?
   b. Is process performance managed?
   c. Are sufficient resources allocated to each process?
   d. Are the interfaces between process steps being managed?

At the job/performer level, the following model highlights the relevant goals, design, and management performance variables:

1. Goals performance variable:

    a. Are job outputs and standards linked to process requirements, which are in turn linked to customer and organizational requirements?

2. Design performance variables:
    a. Are process requirements reflected in the appropriate jobs?
    b. Are job steps in a logical sequence?
    c. Have supportive policies and procedures been developed?
    d. Is the job environment ergonomically sound?

5. Management performance variables:
    a. Do the performers understand the job goals (the outputs they are expected to produce and the standards they are expected to meet)?
    b. Do the performers have sufficient resources, clear signals and priorities, and a logical job design?
    c. Are the performers rewarded for achieving the job goals?
    d. Do the performers know if they are meeting the job goals?
    e. Do performers have the physical, mental, and emotional capacity to achieve the job goals?

By considering the nine performance variables, both in the analysis of the three levels (organizational, process, and job/performer) and in the implementation of process improvement, the OBM practitioner can better meet the overall goals and objectives of the performance improvement efforts.

Process mapping 101 (how to)

Now we get into the world of process mapping 101 (how to). This action is the P in SIPOC (the work process), where OBM practitioners go deep into the steps in a process—what it "is" and what it "should be."

In practice, the following 15 steps help the OBM practitioner work through process mapping:

1. Identify what the process **is**
2. Identify the scope (what's in/out)
3. Identify your swim lanes (who are the "who")
4. Write each step of the process on a post-it note
5. Place the post-it on the wall after each task is identified
6. Repeat until the IS map is complete
7. Take a picture, or write it down

8. Identify areas of improvement
9. Use a different-colored post-it to identify the SHOULD BE map or action plan
10. Think about each step carefully—what you can eliminate, change, add, or keep
11. Take another picture
12. Digitize the map
13. Show map to team
14. Get approval
15. Program for changes!

Here is a quick example of a process-mapping exercise related to onboarding new hires. In this process map, I served as the facilitator and the SMEs were individuals from the recruitment team, new hire training, HR, and supporting departments. Each individual was handed post-it notes to document each step of the task. As each step was documented, participants worked together to ensure the accuracy and the sequencing of the step. This work created the IS map. The team was then asked to identify gaps in the process, bottlenecks in the process, and missing steps. By doing so, the team could not only identify multiple issues with the IS way but also define action steps for the SHOULD BE map.

WHAT ARE TAYLOR'S FOUR PRINCIPLES?

1.	
2.	
3.	
4.	

WHAT ARE THE SEVEN PRINCIPLES/DIMENSIONS OF BEHAVIOR, AS DESCRIBED BY BAER, WOLF, AND RISLEY (1968)

1.	
2.	
3.	
4.	
5.	
6.	
7.	

COMMON DIAGNOSTIC TOOLS IN THE OBM LITERATURE

1. *Observe work in action.*
2. *Listening to your stakeholders looking for performance improvement is equally critical.*
3. *Asking really good questions to get stakeholders involved in the process*

In your own words, describe the common OBM diagnostic tools listed below.

ABC analysis

PDC

Process mapping

OBM REQUIRES ENGAGEMENT

Photo by fauxels from Pexels

Engagement is not a buzz word; rather, it is an action with intention for outcomes. For the manager, engaged employees work hard, strive for great results, and do so with focus and agility to make things happen. For the OBM practitioner, engagement of the stakeholders to ensure a successful OBM initiative is key. Literature on the subject matter of employee engagement in the field of OBM has proven useful in looking at the environment and context of how engagement happens.

Timothy Ludwig and Christopher Frazier (2012) wrote an article titled "Employee Engagement and Organizational Behavior Management" that distilled the critical variables to employee engagement: reinforcement, adequate resources, autonomy, management behaviors, and experimental causality.

Reinforcement: "Perhaps engagement is the label for the classically conditioned response to the copious amount of social and other reinforcement associated with value-added behavior" (Ludwig & Frazier, 2012, p. 78).

Adequate resources: "Availability of resources serves as an antecedent to promote behaviors and to ensure that behaviors are maintained with the proper reinforcers" (Ludwig & Frazier, 2012, p. 78)

Management behaviors: Consistency, communication, and performance feedback are the three management behaviors highlighted to encourage and promote value-adding behaviors (Ludwig & Frazier, 2012, pp. 78–79)

Autonomy: "When managers change the job design to allow for more autonomous behaviors, they may indeed find employees engaging in desirable behaviors beyond the original 'targeted' suggestions" (Ludwig & Frazier, 2012, p. 79).

Experimental causality: "It is easy for organizations to gather data from their employees by giving them surveys that may tell them valuable information… However, it is much more difficult for those organizations to utilize that information for effective behavior change" (Ludwig & Frazier, 2012, p. 79).

For the purposes of providing a starting point for your OBM journey, let us explore influencing the four key stakeholders for any OBM endeavor: colleagues, direct reports, upper management, and yourself as the OBM practitioner.

Whether you're a manager, external consultant, or executive, the following applies.

Engaging Colleagues

There is nothing like working side by side with your colleagues. You each bring something to the table—strengths you can leverage and motivation to make success happen. When it comes to OBM, colleagues are critical to bringing a scientific approach to business as two sets of eyes and ears are better than one. Directly observing behavior in the workplace requires engaging colleagues to validate, confirm, and reinforce what the problem is and whether the solutions are working.

The scientific community calls this collegiate practice *interobserver agreement*, referring to when two or more individuals agree the behavior is happening, or not happening, and whether the solution being implemented to solve the problem is working the way it's supposed to be working. When colleagues are engaged, the science of OBM takes form quickly. Looking at the intricacies of human behavior requires colleagues to work together, observe behavior in real time, and analyze the data toward making decisions.

One thing to pay attention to with colleagues is their motivation in working with you and on the OBM strategy. In most cases, colleagues are in it to win it with you. They have the same focus and passion, the same interest in achieving results. However, some colleagues have other motives. They are looking to be promoted, they want a success story as their past efforts failed, or they want to make a move toward a new direction and see working with you as a ticket. Knowing what your colleagues' motives are will help ensure a successful strategy as there is no reason it would not be a win-win scenario regardless of the motive.

When working with colleagues, OBM practitioners must take the time to define roles and responsibilities. This process allows for identifying who is doing what and when and how within an OBM strategy, specifically for those who work together. At the very least, define your roles and responsibilities with colleagues regarding the following aspects:

- Working with senior managers
- Interviewing stakeholders
- Collecting data and engaging in direct observations
- Analyzing data and reporting
- Decision-making
- Recognizing progress and success

When you define roles and responsibilities, everyone is working toward shared goals and results. This idea, of course, applies to direct reports, upper management, and your own behavior, so consider this a tip that applies to all stakeholders.

One last thing about engaging colleagues—share the risks and rewards. OBM is a science predicated on the notion that the data being collected will be your guide. When looking to improve performance, the data should support all decision-making. Once solutions are identified, there is risk involved as it may not be 100% clear whether the solution will work. You and your colleagues are working together to get the success you are looking for, but the risk is ever present. Ensure you and your colleagues understand and share the risks. As for rewards, those should also be shared. If you know the success of your OBM work is being acknowledged by upper management or even an external entity, share the success and acknowledgement with your team. This practice may seem like a silly thing to say, but if you fail to adhere to this message, colleagues may go another direction at the next opportunity—meaning they won't be working with you again.

Engaging Direct Reports

Engaging direct reports has various challenges and rewards worth noting. Direct reports work for you, and they are looking for your direction. If you say the right things, people get motivated and work to achieve. If you say the wrong things, people get frustrated and demotivated, and no results are ultimately achieved. Whether you are an OBM practitioner or a manager applying OBM, your direct reports require your direction, thoughtful understanding of their challenges, and solutions they can apply to be successful. When it comes to OBM specifically, you are likely asking direct reports to do things differently in their everyday work. That ask means there is a change, and for most, change is hard and scary.

Engaging direct reports has four main essentials for you to consider: (a) direction, (b) protocols, (c) knowledge and skills, and (d) reinforcement.

Direction sets the tone for what the work to be done is, how it should be done to maximize results, and what the desired goal and results are to achieve. Direction is the very start to OBM—*What is the problem to solve? Why is it important? How will success look like? Who will do what and by when?* All these questions provide clear direction.

Protocols are essential to ensure the job gets done the way it is intended to get done. Imagine a job without any procedures, and at the end, what we do in business is ultimately client-facing and can make or break your business. Protocols help employees do the job, do it well, and do it right each time they do it. Without such protocols, the work is being done based on experience, which does not always turn out to be the best way.

Knowledge and skills are critical to the success of any job. Without the right know-how and how-to, employees could be set up for failure. In an OBM strategy, employees need the knowledge and skill to make things happen. Training strategies in the field of OBM are well-documented and well-researched. In brief, organizations who provide employees with the proper training to achieve high levels of fluency in the desired skills will be able to see the return on that investment (Binder, 1997).

Engaging Upper Management

Those in upper management, from directors to executives, are absolutely essential for the success of an OBM strategy. Strategic direction provides the foundation for every OBM strategy. Increasing revenue and market share; improving productivity and efficiency through advanced technologies, mergers, and acquisitions; engaging consumers; and realizing cost savings are all driven from upper management's strategic direction. Typically, the problem OBM practitioners are trying to solve is initiated and defined by the upper management of the organization. Whether you're an external consultant or an internal change agent, upper management starts the conversation of mapping out the problem and the success criteria—which helps you be successful.

Upper management in an OBM strategy has three main roles and responsibilities. First, they set the direction, as previously mentioned. Second, they approve the resources to make it happen. Third, they make the decisions on making any adjustments to the original plan based on data, decisions on moving forward with faster and larger scale, and decisions on whether success has been achieved. These three upper management behaviors cannot be emphasized enough. The OBM practitioner works with upper management to demonstrate these behaviors, provide the data to make decisions, and move the OBM strategy forward.

One last thing about upper management: they must be well-informed along the way. If the OBM strategy is set to take 6, 9, or 12 months or more, remember that OBM is about behavior change, and for organizations, that means a lot of employees making changes to achieve business results. During each week and month that passes, OBM practitioners take time and dedicate attention to keeping upper management informed. Information in an OBM strategy has five core elements:

1. The scope of the work (problem defined, goals, timeline, milestones, success criteria).
2. Data (value-adding behaviors, accomplishments, and business outcomes).
3. Feedback from stakeholders.
4. Implementation of the OBM strategy (progress, obstacles, etc.).
5. Next steps for the OBM strategy, including its sustainability.

The OBM practitioner works with upper management to review this information, discuss it to the point of making decisions, and move the strategy along toward success.

Engaging Yourself

If you're the OBM practitioner or a manager leading the strategy, you are a vital part of the equation for success. Your focus, effort, and drive to make the OBM strategy work are predicated on the notion that you are in fact engaged to make it happen. How do you engage yourself in anything you want to do? How does your environmental setup encourage and maintain your motivation? Think about losing weight, breaking a bad habit, or completing that to-do list that never seems to end—how do you make it happen? In short, engaging yourself in the process of implementing OBM strategies requires an ample amount of clear direction, goals, measures of your progress, and encouragement in the form of experiencing those accomplishments. Imagine devoting a ton of time to any project or initiative only to experience zero accomplishments. How long will your motivation last?

Engaging yourself in the science of human behavior has two parts: self-management and self-feedback. Self-management is all about the discipline of looking at your own behavior, managing both your time and activity level, paired with ample encouragement for getting things done. Self-management takes a life of its own and involves tracking your behaviors and accomplishments, setting goals, and then evaluating progress along the way. Self-feedback is a bit of a double click to self-management, where encouragement and evaluating your progress become about giving yourself feedback on your behaviors. What are you doing well? What should you stop doing? What should you start doing? Simply put, are you doing the very behaviors you need to be doing to experience the accomplishments and end results for which you are striving?

To-do lists, calendar reminders, sticky notes, checklists, and even colleagues are typically used as prompts for self-managing behaviors. Do they work? Of course, they do, but only if they help you achieve the desired accomplishments and outcomes. If not, all you have is a bunch of sticky notes you want to put in the garbage can every day, mostly because they keep piling up. Hopefully, you get the idea. Without proper self-management and self-feedback, you may not be engaging yourself enough to achieve the ultimate success.

IN YOUR OWN WORDS, DESCRIBE THE FIVE VARIABLES TO EMPLOYEE ENGAGEMENT (LUDWIG & FRAZIER, 2012)

For the OBM practitioner, engagement of the stakeholders to ensure a successful OBM initiative is key.

Reinforcement
Adequate resources
Autonomy
Management behaviors
Experimental causality

IN YOUR OWN WORDS DESCRIBE HOW YOU WILL ENGAGE COLLEAGUES, DIRECT REPORTS, AND UPPER MANAGEMENT ON UTILIZING OBM

Engaging colleagues *(You each bring something to the table, strengths you can leverage and motivation to make success happen.)*

Engaging direct reports *(Engaging direct reports has four main essentials for you to consider: (1) direction, (2) protocols, (3) knowledge and skills, and (4) reinforcement.)*

Engaging upper management (Strategic direction provides the foundation for every OBM strategy.)

Engaging yourself *(Your focus, effort, and drive to make the OBM strategy work is predicated on the notion that you're actually engaged to make it happen.)*

OBM STRATEGY PLAN

An OBM strategy plan helps to organize the team regarding who will be implementing the strategy and ensures the desired goals are captured from the perspective of each stakeholder group—executives, employees, and/or customers, as each strategy dictates. The strategy is the roadmap, the guide, the very blueprint for the team to stay focused, evaluate progress along the way, and modify the plan as needed based on data. Without a strategy plan, OBM would be left to guessing and uncoordinated planning—which is not at all scientific.

The essentials of the OBM strategy plan will not be a great surprise to you. You've already been reading the details behind the elements of what is captured in the plan:

1. **The problem defined:** Defined from the perspective of every key stakeholder.
2. **The problem value proposition:** Why it matters to the business, to the employees, and to the customers.
3. **The problem analyzed:** Why the problem exists, starting at the highest level and then a detailed analysis through direct observation and data analysis.
4. **The problem solved success criteria:** What it will look like at the end.
5. **The problem solution set:** The set of solutions based on past science and research, determined to be the "right" solutions.
6. **The problem measured:** The key indicators that will be recorded and reviewed regularly by the organization.
7. **The problem resolution plan:** The timeline, milestones, team, and manner of approach to implementing the solution. In short, the project plan.
8. **The problem resolved and spreading the success:** How the team will solve the same problem across the organization or even beyond the business (i.e., dissemination across the industry).

Here are examples of an OBM Strategy Plan – the first example is an HR strategic effort to improve new hire onboarding, the second example is a safety improvement initiative on safe work permit quality.

HR Example: Improve New Hire Onboarding.

Plan Elements   **Example:**

Plan Elements	Example:
1. The problem defined	New Hires (hourly workers) taking too long to get onboarded and prepared, new hires leaving within first 90 days
2. The problem value proposition	"Ready" to work faster gets employees working with customers, getting paid, and increases retention
3. The problem analyzed	"Too many cooks" – handoffs are not efficient between HR and Operations. New hire lacks information on process steps to complete and by when. Organization compensates minimally for new hire onboarding
4. The problem solved success criteria	Duration of onboarding within first 30 days, retention,
5. The problem solution set	Process steps checklist, single point of contact for new hire, and weekly progress updates with HR staff on new hires
6. The problem measured	Number of days to complete new hire onboarding
7. The problem resolution plan	Process flow mapping with cross functional team, checklists designed and tested, and supervisors and HR co-accountable for duration of onboarding
8. The problem resolved and spreading the success	Begin with Operations, move to other functions about achieving success criteria

Safety Example — Improve Safe Work Permit Quality.

Plan Elements	Example:
1. The problem defined	Safe Work Permits (SWP) being completed as a "check the box" activity, injuries and incidents happening in SWP jobs that can be avoided.
2. The problem value proposition	Reduce/eliminate hazards, reduce/eliminate injuries, and incidents, and improve quality of SWP activities (i.e., discussions, hazard recognition, signoffs).
3. The problem analyzed	Lack of knowledge of requirements, SWP documentation lacks information and sign-off requirements, lack of supervision during SWP documentation, and no feedback or accountability to staff prior to entering SWP.
4. The problem solved success criteria	100% SWP's are signed off by supervisor, hazard mitigation implemented prior to work starting, and injuries/incidents reduced.
5. The problem solution set	Modify SWP documentation, provide on the job training and scenario-based learning, prepare supervisors for on the job coaching and feedback.
6. The problem measured	SWP quality auditing, SWP permit signoffs
7. The problem res-olution plan	EHS team provides training and job aides, supervisors update SWP documentation with staff, EHS team conduct auditing post training of all staff.
8. The problem resolved and spreading the success	Begin with High-Risk jobs requiring SWP at location A, move to other locations each week until fully covered across locations (A-H).

Next, we offer a few helpful tips to consider when putting together your OBM strategy plan, from the voice of various OBM practitioners.

How to Determine the Success Criteria of an OBM Project

Remember those seven dimensions described earlier? Just in case you forget, here they are again, briefly:

1. **Applied:** A problem worth solving.
2. **Behavioral:** Behavior as the focus.
3. **Analytic:** Analysis using data.
4. **Technological:** Writing the details.
5. **Conceptually systematic:** Backed by science.
6. **Effective:** It worked, and you can prove it.
7. **Generality:** Replicate, replicate, replicate.

The value proposition of the seven dimensions provides a starting point for a model of determining success with every OBM strategy. In the world of business, a business case for change is a common tool when documenting any change strategy. A common core set of elements in a business case for change is very similar to the seven dimensions. Here, we illustrate the common elements of a business case for change alongside the seven dimensions of OBM to show the parallel:

The purpose for the change	Applied
The end result of the change	Behavioral
The benefits of the change	Analytic
The plan for change	Technological
The basis for the change	Conceptually Systematic
The measures of success	Effective
The plan to spread the change across the company	Generality

Start at the Top! Depending on where you sit in the organizational chart (employee, supervisor, manager, external consultant), your first point for bringing OBM strategies to improve performance is at the very top of the chart. Executives and senior managers set the priorities, establish the direction, and approve whether change happens. Do yourself a favor: if you're not talking to the senior management team members to start your OBM start, stop what you're doing and redirect your focus and time to work side by side with those individuals.

Make sure it is a priority! Most organizations are working on multiple change strategies. Some are small (e.g., minor procedural changes), some are moderately scaled (e.g., process improvements across multiple departments or product changes), and some are large-scale changes (e.g., reorganizations and mergers/

acquisitions). For an OBM strategy plan to work, it must be on the priority list for the organization. You know what the priorities are when you read a memo from the executives, listen to a month-end or quarterly report briefing, or listen around the office of what people are talking about regarding work activities. What people do day in and day out is driven by the direction of the company, namely the priorities that the company sets to achieve those bottom-line results. Set the OBM strategy on the right footing by ensuring the strategy is part of the overall business strategic plans, ensuring it is in fact a priority.

Enlist the team! The OBM practitioner usually does not work alone. Working side by side with a client who is in a management role or working with colleagues, the OBM practitioner is best served when working collaboratively versus independently. To move things forward with your OBM strategy plan, enlist the team of practitioners and clients who will help with moving the strategy along. Consider enlisting management team members with decision-making authority, an executive steward who has the eye on the big picture, employees who are SMEs in the change effort who know how the rubber meets the road, and of course, seasoned OBM practitioners who can help mentor and guide you in your OBM start. The team will serve as key leverage points for you and the organization to maximize success.

Avoid the traps. We will keep this to a short list because, quite frankly, there are many traps we simply cannot predict as context drives so much of what happens in an OBM strategic plan. Here's a short list of traps to avoid.

> **No direction.** From the top of the organizational chart to the OBM practitioners themselves, direction for the OBM strategy is critical to the organizations success. The goals need to be set—and clearly defined—from the start. The desired value-adding behaviors must be prioritized, defined, and observable. Milestones should be identified to evaluate progress along the way. Not to mention, roles and responsibilities should be delineated, again from the executive team to the employees engaged in the OBM strategy.

> **No data.** A lack of data is no excuse for not gathering data. If there is no data, start gathering some, even auditing, to get a sense of what's happening.

No steward. Priorities do change constantly, but if the organization is intent for the OBM strategy to happen, then an executive team member should be sponsoring the work.

No employee involvement. Limited to no employee involvement is a big mistake. Employees have a great deal of insight into day-to-day operations. The engagement of employees in an OBM strategy can accelerate change, provide useful feedback for improvements, and serve as the main source of positive consequences for all who are involved in implementing the change.

No accountability. Everyone needs accountability in business. Executives are accountable to the board of directors, shareholders, customers, and employees alike. Employees are accountable to the day-to-day operations, customers, and supervisors. OBM practitioners are equally accountable as their clients for the success of the strategies. If you work within a company, your accountabilities may be clear and defined. If you work externally as a consultant, your accountability is three-fold: to the client who makes decisions, to the client who you work with to implement the strategy, and to both the process and outcomes of the work itself. You are only successful if the client is successful. Therefore, ensuring clear accountabilities are in place is an absolute must.

No organizational systems. Ongoing feedback systems, HR infrastructure, operational processes, and corporate policies are needed for the long-term viability of an OBM strategy. When success is realized from implementing OBM, the focus must be on the long-term gains and maintenance of the work that achieved the success. The organizational systems play a major role in the long-term gains.

The components to an OBM strategy plan

An OBM strategy plan helps to organize the team who will be implementing the strategy and ensure the desired goals are captured from the perspective of each stakeholder group—from executives to employees, to customers (if applicable). The strategy is the roadmap, the guide, the very blueprint for the team to stay focused, evaluate progress along the way, and modify as needed based on data. Without a strategy plan, OBM would be left to guessing and uncoordinated planning—not at all scientific.

Below document your OBM strategy plan using the elements provided.

The problem defined
The problem value proposition
The problem analyzed (ABC Analysis, PDC, Process Mapping)
The problem solved success criteria
The problem solution set
The problem measured
The problem resolution plan
The problem resolved and spreading the success

HELPFUL TIPS TO CONSIDER WHEN FORMULATING YOUR OBM STRATEGY PLAN

1. *Your first point of bringing OBM strategies to improve performance is at the very top of the chart.*
2. *For an OBM strategy plan to work, it must be on the priority list for the organization.*
3. *The OBM practitioner will never work alone.*

THE SHORT LIST OF TRAPS TO AVOID WITH YOUR OBM STRATEGY PLAN

No direction. From the top of the organizational chart to the OBM practitioners themselves, having direction for the OBM strategy is critical. The goals need to be set from the start, and they need to be clearly defined. The desired value-adding behaviors must be prioritized, defined, and observable. Milestones should be identified to evaluate progress along the way. Not to mention, roles and responsibilities must be delineated, again, from the executive team to the employees engaged in the OBM strategy.

No data. A lack of data is no excuse for not gathering data. If there is no data, start gathering or even auditing some to get a sense of what's happening.

No steward. Priorities change constantly, but if the organization is really intent on the OBM strategy happening, then an executive team member should be sponsoring the work.

No employee involvement. Having only limited to no employee involvement is a big mistake. Employees have a great deal of insight into day-to-day operations. The engagement of employees in an OBM strategy can accelerate change, provide useful feedback for improvements, and be the main source of positive consequences for all who are involved in implementing the change.

No accountability. Everyone needs accountability in business. Executives are accountable to the board of directors, shareholders, customers, and employees alike. Employees are accountable to the day-to-day operations, customers, and supervisors. As OBM practitioners, we are as equally accountable for the success of the strategies as our clients. If we work within a company, our accountabilities may be clear and defined. If we work externally as a consultant, our accountability is three-fold: to the client who makes decisions, to the client who we work with to implement the strategy, and to both the process and outcomes of the work itself.

We are only successful if the client is successful. Ensuring clear accountabilities are in place is therefore an absolute must.

No organizational systems. Ongoing feedback systems, HR infrastructure, operational processes, and corporate policies are needed for the long-term viability of an OBM strategy. When success is realized from implementing OBM, and note that we said when not if, the focus must be on the long-term gains and maintenance of the work that achieved the success. The organizational systems play a major role in the long-term gains.

BEYOND THE BASICS

Photo by Alex Andrews from Pexels

As the chapter title suggests, you are now beyond the basics. You have knowledge and some know-how in OBM. You may have a burning desire to work with managers and executives across various industries, or work within an organization to be the change agent for all employees and customers. You want to bring the science of OBM and make a positive difference. This course is the first of its class, an opportunity to develop skills to position yourself as an OBM practitioner and to do so with a high degree of integrity for the science.

You won't find this course in any university, and even the largest consulting firms won't share their secrets. Our mission is to grow the field of OBM, to grow the supply and demand, and that growth requires more OBM practitioners. We want more practitioners out in the world serving clients and bringing OBM with a high degree of professionalism. We want you to go beyond the basics and be an OBM practitioner.

We must start with what we mean by *beyond the basics*. The Level 1 White Belt covered the following core elements of OBM (no need to review again, just the list is needed):

- Behavior
- Antecedents
- Consequences
- Employee behaviors vs. leadership behaviors
- The value of data
- Organizational systems
- The role of performance feedback

Now let's look at OBM literature and review beyond these core concepts.

Reinforcement, Positive and Negative Reinforcement

Think about where you work, the people you work with, and the expectations of performance that surround you. What behaviors are people doing every day in your workplace?

- Answering customer phone calls?
- Packaging goods to be shipped to the customer?
- Delivering a service to the customer?
- Managing an audit for the company?
- Developing a strategic plan?

Have you ever wondered why some behaviors happen automatically, why some behaviors occur at higher rates than others, or why some behaviors are not happening at all or maybe only at the minimum level or standard and nothing more? We see it all the time—salespeople upselling, customer service representatives taking additional time with a customer to ensure all needs are met, and nurses keeping a family informed of their loved one's condition. The name of this behavior science game is *reinforcement.*

Reinforcement is a common term, but a very specific definition applies in the world of behavior analysis. Reinforcement is sometimes used as a verb ("Jane is reinforcing Johnny"), an adjective ("Jane is reinforcing to Johnny"), or even a noun ("The ball is a reinforcer"). Behavior analysis defines reinforcement differently to emphasize the occurrence, non-occurrence, and repeated occurrence of behavior. We already discussed antecedents, behaviors, and consequences, and the ABC model that helps us understand the relationship of these three terms. Now, add in the occurrence, non-occurrence, and repeated occurrence of behavior after that first experience with a consequence. Then we can begin to further analyze how much the consequence affects behavior, namely reinforcement.

Imagine you worked all day on your own, in an office, and when the end of day arrived, you realized something—You did not finish a single thing. You resolved no customer inquiries. And you did not even get to have lunch. That day taught you something: whatever you did do did not provide a positive set of consequences. Would you perform the same behaviors the next day? Probably not. It is more that you will want the next day to be a lot better. And to achieve such a day, you will likely need to engage in new behaviors. So now imagine the next day, the one where you prioritized your work tasks, focused on a top-three set of tasks, and completed those before the end of the day. You even got positive feedback from your boss. Would you repeat the same behaviors again on subsequent days? I bet you would.

When behavior maintains at steady rates, or even increases, behavior analysis shows that the behavior is greatly influenced by those consequences. Therefore, reinforcement is occurring. Reinforcement is defined based, again, on the occurrence, non-occurrence, and repeated occurrence of behavior—not to be confused with internal states or feelings of consequences (e.g., "that reward was very positive to me" or "that reprimand was very negative to me"). Reinforcement is not about what something feels like to the individual per se, but rather whether the experience of the consequence influence is enough for the behavior to be maintained, to reoccur, or to stop all together. If behavior reoccurs, reinforcement is happening.

Now, think about those value-adding behaviors discussed in the White Belt—do you want those reoccurring? Of course. To ensure the reoccurrence of behavior happens, reinforcement must be happening. The important variable of behavior is what makes OBM so unique in perspective, application, and science—you know that behavior goes where reinforcement flows (Daniels, 2001). The most powerful type of reinforcement is termed *positive reinforcement* (Daniels, 2016). Positive has a dual meaning—the behavior is maintaining and most likely increasing, and the consequences were added to encourage the behavior to reoccur, meaning a planned consequence (e.g., rewards, recognition). Leaders are coached by OBM practitioners to unlock the application of consequences to reinforce behavior, meaning leaders in organizations can create situations for positive reinforcement to occur.

On the other hand, *negative reinforcement* is defined as the behavior maintaining because consequences support the person avoiding or escaping a negative consequence. Consider a headache. What do you take when you have a headache? Medicine for headaches, right? Maybe a nap. You won't take more medicine without a headache, or more naps even, but you will take more medicine when a headache occurs again to simply maintain a headache-free head. In the workplace, why show up to a meeting on time? To avoid being late perhaps and, in the worst case, to avoid a boss who reprimands people for being late. Either way, negative reinforcement is the impact of consequences to maintain behavior by virtue of avoiding or escaping any potential negative consequences. The focus for the OBM practitioner, which may not come as much of a surprise, is the use of positive reinforcement.

The following are examples of reinforcement for performance.

Behavior reoccurs following positive consequences - Positive Reinforcement.

- Conducting Safe work observations.
- Provided a peer feedback on their safe work practices.
- Stopping a job due to imminent unsafe work conditions.
- Mentoring an employee to grow professionally.
- Contributing ideas to the values of the organization.
- Participating in voluntary employee activities.

Behavior maintains to avoid negative consequences - Negative Reinforcement

- Wearing PPE – mandatory and essential.
- Attendance at work.
- Completing safe work permits.
- Following attendance policies.
- Completing annual refresher training.

Schedules of Reinforcement

With the application of positive reinforcement comes a tricky part of managing performance—how do you best deliver such an experience to people to encourage the value-adding behaviors? The answer lies in understanding schedules of reinforcement (Daniels & Bailey, 2014). *Schedules of reinforcement* are the mechanisms you apply to deliver consequences. The schedules are categorized as follows:

	Interval	**Ratio**
Fixed	• A set time when consequences are delivered	• A set number of occurrences of behavior when consequences are delivered
	Examples • Weekly project team meetings when progress is reviewed • Monthly recognition • Quarterly performance-based pay • Annual promotions	Examples • Number of sales • Number of customer inquiries completed • Number of people trained
Variable	• Varying the time when consequences are delivered	• Varying the number of occurrences when consequences are delivered
	Example • On average, every 2 weeks some gets a bonus	Example • On average, every fifth sale someone gets a bonus

Whatever the schedule, keep in mind the frequency which a reinforcer is administered can affect whether the behavior is strengthened, maintained, or weakened (Latham & Huber, 1991).

If you're looking to provide a positive experience to an employee or fellow colleague for demonstrating those value-adding behaviors, you're a "consequence provider"—an individual providing a consequence. Regarding value-adding behaviors, those consequences (e.g., a thank you, recognition, reward, etc.) are positive ones for the individual. The delivery mechanism should be thought out to ensure the behavior continues. Depending on practicality, it may be more efficient and yet maintain a high degree of effectiveness to provide the consequence on a fixed interval—once a week, once a month, and so on. If the behaviors occur frequently but you need a specific amount of behavior (number of orders filled, number of hours billed, number of sales, etc.), then a fixed ratio would be most prudent.

Behavioral science teaches us that a variable delivery of consequences, both interval and ratio, maintains higher rates of behavior compared to fixed, but monitoring the variability requires a bit more management.

Graph of Schedules of Reinforcement

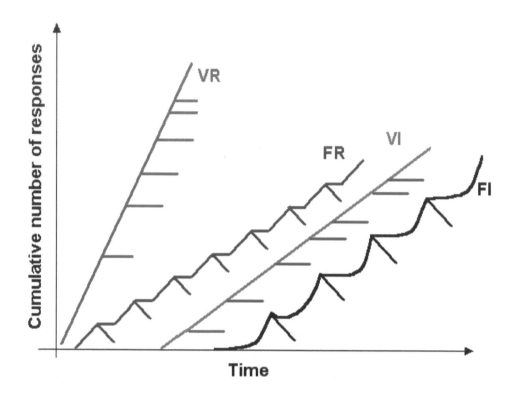

Image source:
https://commons.wikimedia.org/wiki/File:Schedule_of_reinforcement.png

Both lab and applied research has taught us many aspects to consider regarding schedules of reinforcement. As an OBM practitioner, you should factor in five elements when choosing the right schedule of reinforcement:

1. **The environment is ever changing.** Unlike a lab where the environment is controlled, in the business context, most employees move day to day and week to week from task to task. The environment being ever changing may cause a challenge for certain schedules of reinforcement. The manager

must consider when and how often reinforcement can be delivered in day to day business.

2. **Learning and reinforcement histories**. Every employee will have unique work histories, histories of reinforcement, and preferences. Understanding what would be reinforcing for your employees is paramount to your success.

3. **Rules matter.** When behavior is left to guessing whether a positive consequence will actually happen, things are left to chance. While the lab has specific rules at play, in the workplace, the more specific the connection between behavior and consequences, the more likely you will achieve those value-adding behaviors.

4. **Types of reinforcers matter.** What people like may vary from person to person. Some OBM practitioners believe focusing on monetary rewards as reinforcers is prudent as money is used in exchange for what people really want (i.e., food, clothing, time with family). Other OBM practitioners focus on using other reinforcers, such as recognition. Ultimately, identifying what people will perform for (what consequences will be reinforcing) is critical to ensuring behavior happens.

5. **Satiation**. Sometimes what once was a reinforcer (money) may no longer be a reinforcer ("I don't need more money"). For some, money will always be a reinforcer, but the amount of behavior (work) that one must perform to experience the positive consequence must actually be positive and worth the effort. Satiation happens when people receive the reinforcer and no longer "need" it or see value in it; they have had enough. Satiation is common with food: Food is good if someone isn't full, but once they're full, the food is no longer reinforcing.

Hantula (2001) said it best: "The accumulated knowledge of schedules of reinforcement is among the most important features of the distinctive and distinguished contribution that behavior analysis can make to understanding and managing behavior in organizations" (p. 141).

How to pick the "right" schedule of reinforcement

Honestly, it depends! That's a consultant's answer to almost everything, isn't it? But truly, it does depend on what you're looking to achieve. If what you want is for behavior to increase in the future, or the likelihood of behavior to increase in the future, then a positive consequence is needed. In fact, you'd want a behavior so reinforcing that it encourages the behavior to occur again in the future. In this case, you may want a variable ratio of reinforcement, so an average on how often the behavior occurs determines when the positive consequence is delivered.

Below are different schedules of reinforcement in action:

> If you want behavior to maintain at a specific level, then a **variable interval** may be your best bet—so on an average of 6 weeks for recognition and a reward to be given for performance (e.g., positive feedback, public recognition).

> If you are okay with procrastination, meaning you're comfortable that the behavior will occur more often right before the reinforcement is made available, go with a **fixed interval**, which is probably the most practical and easiest to deliver as it is fixed on some time period (e.g., paychecks, bonuses, etc.).

> If you want to reinforce a certain amount of behavior and are "okay" with some drop of performance that then increases closer to receiving the reinforcement, a **fixed ratio** is the best option (e.g., number of orders filled, number of sales completed, number of customer inquiries). The goal remains the same, but a sudden drop in performance is okay if the performer hits the goal.

> If you want to reinforce a behavior and have it stay steadily increasing over time, a **variable ratio** is the best option—for example, with packaging goods or doing data entry—for behavior that happens so frequently that reinforcement can be provided/delivered variably while still sustaining performance at high rates.

Measurement

Photo by Marta Longas from Pexels

The importance of measuring behavior and results cannot be overstated. The field of behavior analysis prides itself on **the use of data and analytics as part of achieving behavior change**. In the world of business, the use of data is critical to monitoring performance—remember, **performance = behavior + results**. The challenge for businesses is making decisions effectively. In fact, one of the toughest challenges for supervisors, managers, and executives alike is the decision-making, as the questions below help highlight:

- Do I have data?
- Do I have the right data?
- Do I have all the data I need to make the right decision?
- Did I make the right decision?

Measurement becomes the true differentiator for the OBM practitioner. With good data comes good decision-making. Through what's sometimes referred to as *data-driven decision-making* (DDDM), the OBM practitioner works diligently with clients and colleagues alike to ensure the "right data" and measurement system is in place to support performance improvement. In business, data helps drive the business and provides insights, which leads to action (Marr, 2016). For professionals with ethical guidelines or codes, effective data collection and data-based decision-making are typically part of their respective practice.

"To begin, data do not objectively guide decisions on their own—people do, and to do so they select particular pieces of data to negotiate arguments about the nature of problems as well as potential solutions." (Spillane, 2012)

If we were to analyze data-based decision-making from an antecedent—behavior—consequence perspective, we may conclude the following:

Antecedents	Behaviors	Consequences
Need for a decision	Gathering data	Right decision
A" Burning issue", ongoing business, new ideas	Reviewing data	Wrong decision
	Listing all possible decisions including past ones (not a common behavior)	Mixed opinions
Past performance (data)		New data presents new decisions to be made
Past decisions (data)		

This analysis is simple in form but complex in solutions as gathering data, reviewing data, and identifying decisions are met with a mix bag of consequences. Continuing with a behavior analysis of decision-making, a few things are worth noting. The sequence of events leading to the decision presents critical variables in the analysis of decision-making processes. Decision-making is typically observable as a persistence and escalation tactic based on reinforcement histories and sequential patterns, versus personal characteristics. In other words, you are likely to make decisions based on some pressing need. In short, you should analyze what decisions are made and how decisions are made in relation to time.

Marr (2016) provides 10 simple steps for any business regarding DDDM:

1. Start with strategy
2. Focus in on the business area
3. Identify your unanswered business questions
4. Find the data to answer your questions
5. Identify what data you already have
6. Work out whether the costs and effort are justified
7. Collect the data

8. Analyze the data
9. Present and distribute the insights
10. Incorporate the learning into the business

Spillane (2012) also provides a way to evaluate data in practice:

> First, look at organizational routines: "specific actions, by specific people, in specific places and at specific times" (Spillane, 2012).
>
> Second, with regard to data, pay attention to what you and others look at daily, weekly, monthly, quarterly, and annually. You're driving decisions by virtue of what you attend to.

From the field of OBM, there are three essentials to using data to make decisions.

First, **data should be over time versus static.** Because you're interested in behavior change to achieve positive business outcomes, data must be evaluated over a period of time. Static data is useful if the intention is to see a comparison point, such as this year versus last year, or one group's performance compared to another group. To manage performance and effectively determine whether things are going in the right direction, ongoing data is critical. When it comes to managing behavioral data, daily or weekly data tracking is common, but sampling through direct observation also works if the sampling is conducted routinely enough.

Second, **data should be clearly understandable**. In some cases, data is displayed in tables, with multiple rows and columns, combining a series of data points into one report. Each row is data needing to be reviewed and analyzed. Of course, data in tables becomes the backbone of good data visualization, but what happens in practice is the table itself becomes the focus point. As a result, much of the data is ignored, and the focus on the data points of interest to the reader, meaning "*I'm looking at this row because that's what I have control over*" or "*these rows are not critical*." This focus becomes problematic as the table then has no real value. For the OBM practitioner, the data should be clearly understandable so that anyone can "get it" and more so analyze the data. OBM practitioners will take data and illustrate the data using a line graph or a bar chart for a given data set. Each data point graphed provides data over time and the opportunity to review and analyze it for trends, variability, and progress against a goal.

Third, **data should result in actions**. When data is presented, reviewed, and analyzed, simply put, it shouldn't just be left at "review and analysis." Rather, the data should lead to some decision and actions! Consider the following questions:

- What should a positive data trend show to progress to a goal trigger?
- How about a negative trend?
- What happens when you reach the goal?
- What do you do when there is significant variability?
- What if the trend is simply staying steady, but that's what you want?

Actions related to data review and analysis typically fall in four categories:

1. Do nothing—keep tracking data.
2. Change how you're working as the data is not going in the right direction—you can't keep repeatedly doing the same thing (insanity definition).
3. Give positive feedback, celebrate early—things are going in the right direction. You may not have hit the goal yet, but you're on your way. Do not wait to recognize such progress. Early celebrations help keep the momentum.
4. Celebrate—you hit your goal, the team worked hard, and it's time to make a big deal of the effort performed.

Three Questions to Ask When Analyzing DDDM Practices

1. **Do you have the "right" information?** There is no such thing as "enough" data, you can always gather more. The "right" information should be available, accessible to the performer, relevant to the problem we are looking to solve, and there should be plenty of data to review for analysis.

2. **Do you have the "right" people to analyze the data?** Having more people is not always needed. Typically, we see discussions with data involved will include subject matter experts, employees and supervisors, senior staff members, and even external consultants. The question becomes "do we have too many people" and not enough "problem solvers?" The "right" people help to analyze, interpret, and get to actions regarding the data.

3. **Do you have the authority to make decisions based on the data, or do we recommend to decision makers?** Authority has a level of accountability and the people in the room must have a level of authority to make decisions or at a minimum, recommendations for the decision makers. Too

often data is reviewed by individuals who care about the data but do not have the level of authority to make decisions nor have a positive history of recommending actions.

My colleagues and I defined a data collection process for the OBM practitioner (Rodriguez et al., 2016, Volume 1). Practitioners have found these 10 elements to support them and their clients to ensure an effective measurement system. I have modified it some from the original work to form questions.

1. What is the pinpoint, the value-adding behavior being focused on?
2. Are you measuring behaviors, results, or both?
3. Will it be measured as an individual or team performance?
4. How will the data be collected and recorded?
5. Who will collect the data?
6. Who will convert the data into meaningful, easy-to-understand information (e.g. graphs, reports, memos)?
7. How frequently will the data be collected, recorded, and summarized?
8. Who will review the data and discuss successes and opportunities for improvement?
9. How often will review of the data and discussions of successes and opportunities for improvement occur?
10. How will the data be communicated across the business, specifically to the key performers?

Without data, you're not doing OBM. Consider this as you continue your journey as an OBM practitioner. Leave nothing to guessing.

Scorecards

Photo by Christina Morillo from Pexels

Following the subject of measurement, one of the most consistent tools used by OBM practitioners and clients alike is the performance scorecard.

A scorecard is a tool to look at several key performance indicators (KPIs) related to the performer's work. Everyone has experienced a scorecard in some form or fashion. School report cards are a form of a scorecard. Athletes get their stats in the form of a scorecard, such as baseball players' hits, runs, walks, batting average, and so on. In the workplace, you may get performance reports; some performance appraisals even include multiple KPIs. A scorecard is therefore all about giving information about one's performance.

There are seven key features of the performance scorecard, according to Dr. William Abernathy (1996), who brilliantly laid out the utility of scorecards:

1. Scorecards are a performance improvement tool
2. Scorecards align employee performance goals
3. Scorecards ensure balanced performance
4. Scorecards facilitate cooperation

5. Scorecards are a management information tool
6. Scorecards are a performance management tool
7. Scorecards foster an entrepreneurial workplace

A scorecard in the workplace should be balanced.

At the organizational level, there are seven categories of value for the scorecard:

revenue, cash flow, expenses, productivity, compliance, customer service, and employee satisfaction. Here is an example of various metrics and the association category:

1. Billed hours (**revenue)**
2. Insurance payments received **(cash flow)**
3. Budget versus actual **(expenses)**
4. Utilization **(productivity)**
5. Treatment integrity audit (avg. per week) **(internal regulatory compliance)**
6. Supervision hours **(regulatory compliance)**
7. CEU hours completed **(regulatory compliance)**
8. Social validity/client satisfaction survey results **(customer service)**
9. Employee retention **(employee satisfaction)**
10. Implementation of new data collection software **(productivity)**

From an OBM perspective, the scorecard offers a unique value proposition for three reasons:

1. First, the scorecard provides information about the individual or team performance across several KPIs of value to the organization.
2. Second, the scorecard is an antecedent for supervisors and managers to provide feedback, and in some cases, the individual employee can reflect on their own performance.
3. Third, the scorecard therefore not only acts to the performer's performance (i.e., recognition, coaching, promotions) but also triggers discussions and actions for future performance (i.e., corrective action plans, professional development plans, performance improvement plans, new goals).

Designing scorecards

Designing the scorecard and any performance measurement system should be managed "and improved on the basis of close observation, by knowledgeable managerial participants, and based on how well it depicts the phenomena it purports to represent" (Norreklit et. al., 2008, p. 67).

Daniels (2015) provides a five-step approach to consider to make measuring behavior meaningful:

1. Plan a positive consequence for the activity being measured.
2. Reinforce the behavior without waiting for the result.
3. Consider rewards (incentives, as some call them) necessary but not enough.
4. Make rewards relevant to the performer—know what is reinforcing to the person or variable being measured (e.g., Fitbit Awards Badges would not be a good reinforcer for me—I have no idea how many I have or what they're for).
5. Track behavior since it will provide many more opportunities to positively reinforce improvement, as reflected by the measure.

What Are the Pitfalls of Using a Scorecard?

The implementation and vitality of scorecards are susceptible to various pitfalls, as detailed below.

Oversimplification (Norreklit et al., 2008): A group of measures does not make a business. Managers of the business sometimes change course based on market pressures, customer demands, and so on. The scorecard is ultimately a means to understand the "health" of the business, but if the data is not where you want it to be, there may be external variables influencing the data. The scorecard therefore has a key pitfall to avoid—oversimplification! Keeping things simple is purposeful in utility of the scorecard, meaning not making it too complicated for use, but notations of external variables that influence the data are critical to the usefulness of the scorecard.

The balance of measures (Norreklit et al., 2008): The scorecard model comes from the great minds of Kaplan and Norton (1996), where the goal is to strike a balance of measures related to the performance of interest. Four categories of measures are proposed as the critical focus point for the scorecard: (a) learning and growth, (b) internal business processes, (c) customers, and (d) financial outcomes. The balance within the scorecard is viewed as a potential pitfall of the system—who decides what the balance is? The work of balancing the scorecard with measures that motivate is an intricate part of the process of developing the scorecard itself. Taking the right amount of time, with the right people, and performing ongoing monitoring and modification as needed are central steps to striking the balance.

Misleading cause and effect (Norreklit et al., 2008): Many believe the scorecard provides the cause-and-effect data needed to evaluate the success of the business and strategies for achieving results ("If we improve customer satisfaction, we will see results financially"). This cause-and-effect thinking accounts for neither how results are achieved nor the variables that influence results. Customer satisfaction can be very high without a single sale. Revenue can soar with product sales versus service-oriented delivery. You can also achieve results the wrong way—forcing sales on customers, overpricing goods, and overworking employees, for example. The data should be a guide to understanding both the health of the business and the people side, which makes or breaks the business. KPIs are named as such for a reason; they indicate the key performance areas for the business.

Timing difficulties (Norreklit et al., 2008): Scorecards are designed to organize data, focus on the KPIs, and trigger discussions about the data. Unfortunately, the dimension of "time" related to seeing improvement in those KPIs is typically not well-represented in the scorecard. Scorecards formatted with dates or weeks/months as columns will overcome this challenge. However, caution is still needed by the manager who uses a scorecard bet doesn't pay attention to the improvement strategies supporting those KPIs. In short, some KPIs may need more time than others to show positive results or achieve the desired goals.

Managerial remoteness (Norreklit et al., 2008): The more data in a manager's hands, the more managing from a distance may get reinforced. As Norreklit et al. (2008) stated eloquently, using the scorecard can lead to managers being "detached from the operations for which they are responsible" (p. 67).

What you measure is not always what you get (Norreklit et al., 2008): Similar sayings like "you get what you measure" are familiar. The challenge and pitfall here are, well, that it's simply not true. As Dr. Aubrey Daniels (2015) illustrated brilliantly, "What gets measured improves the chances of getting done." Taking a behavioral science approach to measurement, what Daniels is describing is the connection between what's being measured and how people's behaviors are influenced from the strategies, decisions, and ongoing performance management of the same measurement. In summary, what gets measured leads to managers and employees analyzing the data, discussing the data, and making decisions based on the data to ensure success—bringing the opportunity for positive consequences along the way. What gets measured therefore leads to a greater probability of positive consequences being made available, resulting in a work environment of positive reinforcement.

How Do You Avoid These Pitfalls?

Norreklit et al. (2008) described it very well: treat the "performance measurement system as an explorative and iterative learning approach for management rather than the mechanical learning system that the [balanced scorecard] assumes" (p. 67).

Gligorea (2013) provided additional pitfalls to avoid, but for our purposes, we will translate them into actionable steps to ensure successful implementation.

Measure focus on a clear and comprehensive strategy. The organization's executives develop and approve the strategies to make bottom-line impact. For every employee to understand how they contribute to those strategies, performance measures should be clearly linked. This linkage takes time for the OBM practitioner and who you work with to "follow the breadcrumbs," so to speak, and trace the links. Here is a quick example:

- Bottom-line result: Profit
- Profits: Revenue minus expenses
- Department heads: Manage expense budgets to come out at or below budget
- Customer service and sales departments: Manage sales leads and closure rate to maximize purchase orders and bulk sales
- Accounting department: Collects cash/payments from customers within 30–60 days
- Operations: Maintains order fulfillment time delivery and maintains quality standards (after all, if customers don't get their orders on time and to their expectations, costs go up, and you may lose customers).

Communicate and educate. As with most everything in an organization, employee performance requires not only clarity of the "what and why" but also education to ensure they know the "how." With scorecards, you're measuring employee performance and expecting an outcome. And the proper use of scorecards requires ongoing management, discussions with employees, analysis when problems arise, and celebrations when you meet the goal. With the implementation of scorecards therefore comes the need for communications and education; each and every employee should understand what the scorecard is, why it's important, what the goals are and why they're important, how measures are chosen, and how the scorecard will be used (i.e., regular employee/supervisor meetings, coaching and feedback, performance expectations, celebrations). Education on the scorecard should include practice for both employees and managers on the use of the scorecard. Education is important as the use of the scorecard requires a clear understanding of how to use the scorecard, how not to use the scorecard, and how the scorecard aims to support overall performance improvement.

Accountability. This word sends chills down some people's spines, typically because of its negative connotation and pairing with being in trouble. However, *accountability* truly means ownership of an outcome and how the outcome is achieved. For scorecards, each KPI should have an accountable owner—someone who is ultimately responsible for the success of that performance measure. Accountability is not hard to comprehend: a sales manager should be accountable for sales, an operations director should be accountable for safety and production, an accountant should be accountable for compliance and accuracy of the books. The hard part of accountability is when everyone is accountable, which means no one will be. A single point of accountability provides clear direction and expectation for the individual to "own" that measure and all the things that relate to the performance management system.

Employee empowerment. "Employees must also have the authority, responsibility and tools necessary to impact relevant measures" (Gilgorea, 2013)—we completely agree.

Individual and team-based scorecards. Often the focus of a scorecard is at the organizational level. Bottom-line measures become the focus, one where the performance management of every employee who contributes to the bottom line occurs. By focusing on creating individual and team-based scorecards, and rolling them up to the executive board room, the scorecard and the alignment of measures becomes clear, are linked, and provides relevant information for every employee, manager, and executive.

Leading and lagging measures. A scorecard should have both leading and lagging indicators. A common analogy to describe leading and lagging indicators goes something like this: Leading indicators look forward, like looking through a windshield in a car. Lagging indicators look backward, like looking in your rearview mirror. The question becomes the value and relevance to a measure based on whether it helps you to look backward or look forward. Leading indicators therefore are what you want to support when encouraging the "right" value-adding behaviors and the outcomes of behaviors (accomplishments and results). Business results can be leading indicators, such as customer satisfaction, productivity, and quality. Lagging indicators are important as well; by looking backward, employees have a good understanding of their past performance, which can help them with their future performance, but only if the leading indicators are present as well. For instance, the total profit I was able to generate last month only helps me if I know how many leads, sales, sales closed, and expenses I managed in that same period.

Specific and relevant metrics. Look at the job roles and responsibilities, the day-to-day work, and you know what you'll find? Relevant measures of performance—directly or indirectly stated. This relates to the use of SMART goals (Geller, 2003). A goal is a preset or specified level of performance to be attained. Good goals are SMART goals (Geller, 2003), meaning they're **specific, motivational, achievable, relevant, and trackable.** After defining the goal, managers take great care to ensure they meet the SMART criteria. Testing the criteria requires feedback from those affected by the goals and those who influence the goals. Make the goals and measures associated with the goals specific and relevant.

Pay for Performance

Photo by mentatdgt from Pexels

Pay for performance certainly isn't a new phenomenon. A familiar name to our certification program, Frederick Winslow Taylor, contributed to the history of pay for performance from his use of time studies to identify output standards and individualized incentive plans. Taylor implemented differential piece-rate incentives where those who did not meet the standard were paid a lower rate than those who met or exceeded the standard. The latter were rewarded beyond the base pay.

As a result of Taylor's contribution, many derivatives of incentive plans emerged, with analyses showing two basic types: time wages and wages saved. The Hawthorn studies, one of the most cited studies to date, provided a great deal of scientific evidence on employee performance pay. Unfortunately, over the years, several interpretations of the Hawthorne studies and even the official account suggest that the results are not supportive of incentive payments on performance. Still, the studies have, since their conclusion, unquestionably influenced generations of pay-for-performance.

Parsons (1991) provided a review of the Hawthorne studies from an OBM perspective. First, the focus on collecting data from each participant's behavior was a key element of the studies, which in turn is a core focus for OBM. The use of such data provided the performer feedback, another core element of OBM practice and research. As a result, the studies included a pay contingency resulting in performance improvements.

Dr. William B. Abernathy (1996, 2011) described how his research and practice led to his position and future writings advocating for a "total performance system." A few key points differentiate, and expand, the total performance system from the traditional pay-for-performance models. This model is also what my colleagues and I call *modern pay for performance* (Bucklin et al., 2020) because it's a robust system that encompasses the benefits of the other systems described earlier in this chapter, but eliminates the challenges of those other systems.

The modern pay-for-performance model includes scorecards (balanced performance scorecards) + profit-indexed performance pay + performance management, as shown in the following graphic.

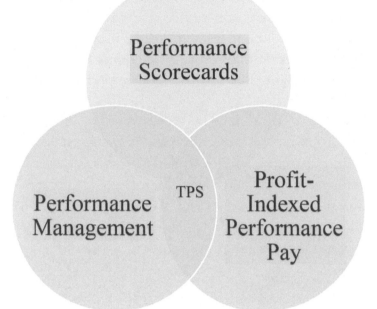

Total performance system illustrated via Venn diagram (Abernathy, 2011)

Balanced performance scorecards. First, having well-designed balanced score-cards across the organization, department, and individual levels eliminates the "one-dimensional" issue with some individual incentive plans.

Profit-indexed performance pay. Abernathy's (2011) solution depended upon a rather complex formula as an indicator of the organization's profitability, in what he called an *organizational multiplier.* Conceptually, this makes sense. If the company is not profitable, then there are no payouts regardless of individual performance scores. If the company achieves its maximum profitability, employees can potentially earn up to three times the organization's established percent of base pay. A deviation from Abernathy's model is a simple profit-sharing approach establishing a static budget available for individual payouts each year, quarter, or month (Bucklin et al., 2020). This solution is transparent to employees with the ability for the organization's leaders to define what will be available as pay for performance based on the individual employee's balanced scorecard result.

Performance management. The performance management element of the total performance system provides a focus on the use of data to evaluate performance, troubleshoot problem areas, and make decisions to implement solutions toward maximizing performance, including the use performance management techniques, such as the ABC analysis (Braksick, 2007; Daniels & Bailey, 2014); diagnostic tools such as Austin's (2000) Performance Diagnostic Checklist, and Mager and Pipe's (1970) problem-solving questions. These techniques coupled with direct observations, data gathering and analysis, and working with organizational management on identifying solutions to implement become a foundational element of performance management. Abernathy (1996, 2011) focused his readers on ensuring a rich feedback loop is established to ensure the other elements of the total performance system will be successful.

Although Abernathy's approach is sophisticated and robust, little empirical research has validated the total performance system in its entirety. While Abernathy provided case examples of each component, illustrating positive results, empirical research would be beneficial for the OBM practitioner as clients' needs and interest in seeing evidence-based approaches are growing.

Pay for Performance in Practice

Considering everything discussed and what's recommended by pay-for-performer gurus (Abernathy, 2011; Daniels & Bailey, 2014), my colleagues and I (Bucklin et al., 2020) identified what ensures the most effective performance-based pay at the individual and organizational level:

- Structured based on company values and strategic objectives
- Agile enough to be updated with changing business needs
- Consideration of both the organization's profit and the individual's performance, which eliminates problems of paying high wages to employees when the organization is experiencing cash flow or profitability shortages
- Focused on employee contributions; used to motivate
- Transparent—meaning that scorecards, measures, and results are shared to set expectations and are aligned with feedback and incentives
- Contingent on an employee's own performance
- Based on clearly specified behaviors or accomplishments
- Certain (i.e., if the performance occurs, the individual will always receive the pay)
- Paid as soon after the performance as possible, or at least linked with frequent feedback

Pay-for-Performance Readiness

My colleagues and I (Bucklin et al., 2020) have identified some specific readiness needs for organizations when preparing to launch pay-for-performance strategies. If an organization isn't ready, the system can be ineffective at best and detrimental at worst.

> Executive and management readiness. Executive and senior leaders need to spend time identifying organizational-level results aligned with their business strategies. They must "own" the scorecards. Manager and supervisor buy-in are also crucial for pay-for-performance to be successful. For many organizations, this type of system changes the behaviors required by managers and supervisors, which may be time-consuming and aversive at first. It's up to executive leaders to create and deliver positive consequences for their managers and supervisors, contingent on engaging in those new behaviors.
>
> IT systems. For scorecards to function most effectively, the organization must have IT systems in place to collect data and populate scorecards.
>
> Systems for sharing scorecard results. The more frequently and easily employees and their managers or supervisors can view current scorecard data, the more effective the program will be.
>
> Time allocation for scorecard work. Managers need time to complete or review their department and employees' weekly, monthly, and/or quarterly scorecards, and to provide feedback to their employees based on results.

Leadership Behaviors

Photo by fauxels from Pexels

Leadership is the process of influencing others (Vroom & Jago, 2007). Influencing others requires behavior, context, and an end goal. Ultimately, leadership is an umbrella term like personality (Krapfl & Kruja, 2015). In the field of OMB, much has been written about regarding the leadership construct because, in action, leadership plays a critical role in the success of any organizational change effort.

Krapfl and Kruja (2015) described a "leadership behavior menu" serving as a list of behavior classes identified as "valuable for most leaders" (p. 31).

A value proposition: More than a vision, the leader offers a value proposition that has a reciprocal relationship—such as reinforcement for the organization and the consumer.

Ethical values: Integrity and trust are "separate and equally important aspects of ethics" (Krapfl and Kruja, 2015). Both integrity and trust are evaluated by others. The leader following through on commitments, demonstrating honesty, and doing what they say they are going to do are examples of behaviors related to integrity and trust. Although these two aspects are constructs and require context, the impact of a lack of integrity and lack of trust is undoubtedly accepted as something undesirable.

Execution skills: These skills "make things happen" (Krapfl and Kruja, 2015). The rubber meets the road when it comes to an individual's ability to get things done, done well, and done to the satisfaction of stakeholders. A leader's ability to execute plans, simple or complex, is a key skill to develop, practice, and build as a habit.

Communication skills: It should come as no surprise that communication is seen as a valuable behavior for leaders to demonstrate. Krapfl and Kruja (2015) eloquently described "three important, yet often neglected, aspects of effective communication for a leader" (p. 34)—(a) leaders provide employees with both the picture and the details when required, (b) leaders' communications are clear and concise, and (c) leaders listen to be further informed and act upon a great deal of insight and knowledge.

Enabling skills. "Enabling leaders use their position and authority to provide subordinates with opportunities to grow. Rather than taking responsibility directly, an enabling leader or manager delegates responsibility downward, offers support and guidance when requested or deemed necessary, provides feedback and advice, and tolerates error" (Krapfl and Kruja, 2015). Delegation, ensuring resources are provided, and ongoing coaching and feedback are all well-documented leadership behaviors to enable others to perform. "A leader who enables others understands their responsibility is to develop subordinates and recognize[s] that both their personal position and the organization will benefit from that development" (Krapfl and Kruja, 2015).

Team-building skills. "A team differs from a group in that the team must collaborate on a shared objective … [and] the leader's primary task is not necessarily to lead the team himself or herself but rather to select team members based on expertise and past performance in working with others" (Krapfl and Kruja, 2015). Team-building skills are about the leader's ability to foster the team dynamics, encouraging the team to work together versus independently.

Confronting adversity. "Effective leaders are complex problem solvers … In addition to addressing adversity once it has risen, effective leaders constantly monitor the project's progress in order to prevent or prepare for possible problems" (Krapfl and Kruja, 2015). Unfortunately, confronting adversity is typically a role a leader plays as the goal of leadership is to support and influence others toward success. Sometimes to achieve success, you must deal with adversity.

Tenacity. "Effective leaders persist under these conditions and successfully influence others to do the same. Anyone who has implemented a strategy can tell you that, no matter the quality of the strategy, its implementation rarely goes as planned, and confronting unforeseen obstacles is something to be expected as a matter of course" (Krapfl and Kruja, 2015). Consider the analogy of a ship captain, who has a destination. During their course, bad weather approaches on the horizon, and they must deviate course. The captain calls orders to the staff to go off course and avoid the weather. Afterward, the captain calls orders on how to get back on course to reach the desired destination. Tenacity is all about implementing the strategy but also about adjusting to ultimately keep everyone safe, healthy, and productive, helping to ensure they reach their goals.

Culture-building skills. Simply put, culture can be defined as "the way we do things around here" (Krapfl and Kruja, 2015). Staffing, trust, reliability, and continuity of relationships are described as essential for leaders to foster a positive culture. Culture-building is such an important skill that we want to dedicate a few moments on the subject.

Accordingly, we've included the following excerpts, which were originally published by *Business Science Magazine* in December 2019 and written by Manuel "Manny" Rodriguez

The article "Cultural Change That Sticks" offers a great reminder of the power culture has on organizational success (Katzenbach et al., 2012). The authors described five principles to obtaining peak performance. Each of these principles are not for the faint at heart. They require focus, prioritization, and leadership, to name a few necessitates.

First, match strategy and culture. A methodology used in OBM called *behavioral systems analysis* speaks to this very point. In brief, behavioral systems analysis maps out elements of an organization from mission and vision and process cross-functionally to behaviors at the individual contributor level. When challenges are identified, a "multilevel solution" set is designed to tackle individual performance, group performance, process improvement, and organizational strategy; that solution might include policies, resource deployment, and incentive systems, for instance (Diener, McGee, & Miguel, 2009). This approach supports a complete culture change from the organizational level to the individual level. Importantly, "culture is based on the past, whereas strategy tends to focus on the future" (Krapfl & Kruja, 2015).

Second, focus on a few critical shifts in behavior. This principle is taught heavily in the field of OBM (Braksick, 2007; Daniels & Bailey, 2014; Ditzian, 2019). Pinpointing those few behavior changes needed to move the needle in the organization can truly make a significant impact.

Third, honor the strengths of your existing culture. This principle was demonstrated by Aetna's management team in the case study. By focusing on the strengths of the existing culture, you can leverage the very best the individuals and collective group can bring to the proverbial table. This leverage can build significant acceleration to any culture change you embark on utilizing what behavior science calls *behavior momentum*, the strategy of making requests that are easy to perform before making more difficult requests.

Fourth, integrate formal and informal interventions. Interventions come in all shapes and sizes. Restructuring, new policies and procedures, checklists for daily routines, and training are probably all things you have experienced before. Informal interventions are more like what you would see people doing in the break room or by the "water cooler." It is about having conversations to stimulate change without all the fanfare of a corporate meeting, new policy, or training program. These informal interventions can be simple coaching discussions (Gavoni & Weatherly, 2018).

Fifth, measure and monitor cultural evolution. My own familiarity with achieving cultural change from a behavior science perspective corresponds well with principle five, both on measuring and monitoring the culture, and on how culture can evolve over time. Measuring culture has many forms, such as surveys, focus groups, behaviors, and outcomes. The collection of these indicators would be most beneficial to evaluate the culture of an organization and most critical to get the perception of those who work at the company.

Coaching, Deliberate Coaching

Photo by mentatdgt from Pexels

Coaching people to achieve has amazing benefits for all involved—the recipient, the coach, and the organization. When an organization implements a coaching system, the benefits are realized in an exponential improvement in performance. Coaching is a critical skill set for the OBM practitioner.

Deliberate coaching, a term coined by Gavoni and Weatherly (2019), **is a model of behavioral coaching that revolves around precise, purposeful, and systematic coaching interactions. As part of deliberate coaching, the OBM practitioner** is focused on a specific targeted outcome that all employees are accountable to achieve.

One example of this focused coaching comes from the article "Cash Is King!" by Rodriguez (2011), where an Accounts Receivables Team focused on receivables alongside the business development/sales team, executive management team, and customer service team. Each team member received direct coaching from a third party, accelerating their performance and ultimately achieving their goals within months instead of years.

Coaching is a term widely used throughout the English language and means many different things. We hear about players being coached during a game, business owners receiving coaching from other professionals, or individuals receiving coaching in several areas from health and wellness to accountability and time management. However, coaching in behavior analysis is a bit different because it's a process that includes individual observation and feedback with a primary focus on developing task-specific skills within a certain time frame (Gavoni & Weatherly, 2019).

For the purposes of training OBM practitioners, we adopt a definition of coaching described in the article "Coaching as a Packaged Intervention for Telemarketing Personnel" by Tilka and Johnson (2018). Coaching is "an individualized approach consisting of prompting, modeling, and differential evaluative feedback regarding job performance that is provided on an ongoing and frequent basis to employees" (Tilka & Johnson, 2018, pp. 50–51).

Specifically, the coaching process includes the following behaviors:

1. Observation and active listening
2. Feedback
3. Shaping
4. Thinning schedules of reinforcement

"Coaching is most crucial during the early development of a new skill, in which dense and frequent socially mediated positive reinforcers are delivered for incremental improvement" (Gavoni & Weatherly, 2019)

Returning to Gavoni and Weatherly's (2019) definition of *deliberate coaching*, let's review their meaning behind precise, purposeful, and systematic (p. 96-97

Precision coaching is about the following:

- Measuring performance with specificity, details, and high-frequency monitoring
- Distinguishing clearly between the development and transferring of skills
- Providing feedback specific to a pinpointed behavior
- Providing feedback on behaviors linked to results

Purposeful coaching is about the following:

- Ensuring a clear link to on-the-job outcomes

- Designing positive procedures
- Sustaining the focus on a few pinpointed behaviors

Systematic coaching is about the following:

- Applying proven procedures
- Measuring improvements of individuals' performance
- Using data to guide coaching
- Using social validity to monitor and guide coaching

For the OBM practitioner, the coaching skill set evolves over time. For the purposes of this course, we provided a definition of coaching, more specifically deliberate coaching, and now we want to provide some strategies on how to evaluate your coaching efforts.

Thomas (2004) provides five principles you can apply to transform performance:

1. Accurately assess the readiness to change
2. Clearly state the overall strategic direction
3. Identify the key stages in the journey
4. Gain commitment to the common goal
5. Establish a process to learn and grow

When evaluating your coaching efforts, the focus of the evaluation should be on (a) the behavior change itself, (b) the business results change related to the behaviors, (c) satisfaction with coaching (social validity), and (d) what we call *coaching integrity* (whether you follow your process).

One last thing worth mentioning about coaching: there are three categories of people you will encounter as a coach (Thomas, 2004):

1. Individuals who are aligned with the organization. They are "ready, set, go."
2. Individuals who are aligned, but their "needs vs. wants" + motivation compared to the organization's needs may not be aligned completely.
3. Individuals who will demonstrate "discord" to coaching. Are they the right people in the right role at the right time?

Each of these individuals will present themselves throughout your coaching, and each can be supportive of the overall organizational goals, with your coaching supporting their efforts. Coaching, and more specifically deliberate coaching, ensures helping all team members to achieve.

For your coaching to get started on the right track, think about all the individuals and the role you play as a "coach," and then consider the following:

- What are their roles and functions?
- How many people or teams receive coaching?
- How were they selected to receive coaching?
- Did they receive training prior to coaching on any specific skill?
- Is there coaching for you, the coach?
- How will you collect information on the impact of your coaching?
- What evidenced-based practice will you be utilizing?

Educating OBM to Non-OBMers

When you're an OBM practitioner, your differentiator is OBM itself. As part of your practice, you will have several opportunities to teach and educate your colleagues, clients, and the world, really, on what OBM is all about, how it's applied, and it's desired impact. At this point, we want to cover a few techniques to teaching OBM by sharing what has worked for practitioners around the world.

Elevator pitch: Imagine you're in an elevator, train ride, or airplane trip and someone asks "What do you do?" Granted, the elevator trip is much shorter than a train ride or airplane travel, but that's the point. How would you answer the question given those various time frames? The answer is in the practice of your elevator pitch, which might go something like this:

> *What do you do? I'm an OBM practitioner*
> *What is an OBM Practitioner? A scientist for performance improvement in business.*
> *What kind of science? Behavioral science.*
> *What is behavioral science? ...*

By practicing your elevator pitch, you can master the art and precision of clearly communicating the science of making a positive difference in the workplace. The OBM practitioner should have an elevator pitch lasting a few seconds, up to 120-seconds, and a more formal pitch not lasting more than 5 minutes. The idea with the various pitches is to always be prepared with a clear, concise answer to the question "what do you do" for the sole purpose of attracting potential clients.

The 2x2 matrix

The 2x2 matrix, per our description, is a tool to educate our colleagues, clients, and others on some concepts, principles, and so on related to OBM. As stated by Lucid Meetings (2020), "the 2x2 Matrix is a decision support technique where the team plots options on a two-by-two matrix." For the OBM practitioner, the 2x2 is used to illustrate specific points to gain forward momentum on applying OBM and, more specifically, on reaching some conclusion for performance improvement.

Lucid Meetings (2020) explains the following: "Popular 2x2 matrix categories include: Cost and Value, Importance and Urgency (the Eisenhower Box), Time and Money, Effort and Impact, Taste (Great) and Satiety (Less Filling). The 2x2 format is also used for exercises that collect input in four distinct categories, the most famous of which is the SWOT (Strengths, Weaknesses, Opportunities, and Threats) analysis."

A few 2x2 matrices OBM practitioners have used with a great deal of success are shown below:

The Want, Don't Want, Get, Don't Get Matrix.

	Get	Don't Get
Want	• You get what you want. • You more than likely will do it again. • Positive reinforcement	• You don't get what you want. • You more than likely will not do it again. • You may try again. • Extinction.
Don't Want	• You get what you don't want. • You more than likely will not do it again. • Punishment	• You don't get what you don't want. • You avoided or escaped something, so you will keep doing the behavior. • Negative reinforcement

Leadership Behaviors

	Poor impact on others	Positive impact on others
Great Results	• This leader achieves great results but has a poor impact on others. • People don't generally want or like to work with this leader; some would say they actively avoid this individual. • Unfortunately, this leader tends to get promoted because of results.	• This leader has a positive impact on others and achieves business results. • People not only want to work for this leader, but also want others to as well. • This leader is exceptional, sought out, and excel in the long term.
Poor Results	• This leader doesn't achieve results and has a negative impact on others. • This leader doesn't typically "make it," potentially gets fired or moved from leadership roles.	• This leader has a positive impact on others, but it's due to being a "nice person" rather than being an effective leader. • This leader doesn't achieve positive results. • Typically, this leader has a limited scope of accountability but maintains some leadership role as most people will perform to some level of expectations.

Both 2x2 matrices can be used interactively with a group. Asking for examples of getting something you want (recognition) versus getting something you don't want (reprimand) helps to make the point of performance over time.

Another good approach is to come prepared with generic examples, such as getting a speeding ticket (something you get that you don't want) and avoiding a speeding ticket by driving the speed limit (negative reinforcement, not getting something, you don't want). As for the leadership 2x2, you can make that interactive by working with upper management to identify where the "leaders" in the organization fall within the 2x2.

LIST THE SEVEN AREAS OF OBM THAT ARE BEYOND THE BASICS

We began the Yellow Belt with seven key concepts and practice areas of OBM beyond the basics. List them here, and using the space below, write down any takeaways or "a-ha!" moments you may have experienced during the review.

The Seven Areas of OBM That Are Beyond the Basics

1.

2.

3.

4.

5.

6.

7.

MATCH THE DESCRIPTIONS WITH THE TERMS FROM THE SEVEN OBM AREAS BEYOND THE BASICS

Using the definitions provided, list the seven areas of OBM beyond the basics covered in the Yellow Belt. Note, the following are listed out of order from the course to support your learning.

1. REINFORCEMENT, POSITIVE & NEGATIVE REINFORCEMENT

2. SCHEDULES OF REINFORCEMENT

3. MEASUREMENT

4. SCORECARDS

5. PAY FOR PERFORMANCE

6. LEADERSHIP BEHAVIORS

7. COACHING, DELIBERATE COACHING

❑ The use of data and analytics as part of achieving behavior change. Remember, performance = behavior + results.

❑ Certainly isn't a new phenomenon…yet OBM proposes a model that includes scorecards + profit indexed performance pay + performance management.

❑ Plays a critical role in the success of any organizational change effort.

❑ The occurrence, non-occurrence, and repeated occurrence of behavior after the first experience with a consequence.

❑ A model of behavioral coaching that revolves around precise, purposeful, and systematic coaching interactions.

❑ One of the most consistent tools used by OBM practitioners and clients alike related to measurement.

❑ The mechanisms we apply to deliver consequences, includes fixed interval, fixed ratio, variable interval, and variable ratio mechanisms.

IDENTIFY TWO TECHNIQUES FOR TEACHING OBM

When you're an OBM practitioner, your differentiator is OBM. As part of your practice, you will have several opportunities to teach and educate your colleagues, clients, and the world really on what OBM is all about, how it's applied, and its desired impact. What were the two techniques described for teaching OBM? In your own words, identify each technique based on the description provided. We also encourage you to write down any notes that help you in using these techniques.

Technique 1: _____

A means to master the art and precision of clearly communicating the science of making a positive difference in the workplace. Helps answer the following questions: *What do you do? What is an OBM practitioner? What is the science?*

Technique 2: _____

A tool to educate our colleagues, clients, and so on regarding some concepts, principles, etc., related to OBM. It also helps illustrate specific points for us to gain forward momentum on applying OBM and, more specifically, reaching some conclusion for performance improvement.

PROJECT MANAGEMENT ESSENTIALS

To be an OBM practitioner is to be an assessor, an implementer, an evaluator, a manager of people completing tasks and activities to achieve an outcome, and of course, an SME in behavior science. A skill set that supports the OBM practitioner is project management, and for many, this skill is developed over a great deal of time. From one project to another, unique context variables exist for each project. Today, project management is a skill set, a professional career path, a title in an organization (project manager), and a necessity to achieve strategic imperatives.

According to the Project Management Institute (2020), *project management* is "the application of knowledge, skills, tools and techniques to project activities to meet the project requirements." This combination of knowledge, skills, tools, and techniques highlights project management as a skill set, not too far from OBM itself, which is truly a combination of the same variables—knowledge, skills, tools, and techniques. What is great about project management is the application of the skill set scientifically, methodically, and with purpose. Project management and OBM are truly a great match.

There are five phases to a project, and below, we review each phase and provide specifics to consider from an OBM perspective.

Phase 1. Concept and Initiation

In every story, there is a beginning, and for every project, the beginning is conceived and initiated by the organization to either solve a problem, explore new opportunities, or improve something further. Pathak (2020) described this phase in more detail:

A project is formally started, **named, and defined at a broad level** during this phase. **Project sponsors** and other important stakeholders diligently **decide whether to commit to a project**. Depending on the nature of the project, feasibility studies are conducted. Or, as it may require, in an IT project—requirement gathering, and analysis are performed in this phase. In the construction industry a project charter is completed in this phase.

A few key points are worth describing further and provide an OBM perspective. First, naming and defining a project at a broad level during this phase provides the overall direction, vision, and purpose of the project. The broad level may be interpreted as ill-defined, but typically, the broadness of the project definition represents the end goal and the impact the project will have. The broad-level definition will be further defined in the second phase; however, from an OBM perspective, the end goal must be clearly defined, including how it will be measured and evaluated.

Second, the role of a project sponsor is very important to the overall success of the project. This individual will represent the senior management team regarding the project and will ultimately be held accountable. The project sponsor can be very involved in the project or far removed in the day to day. Regardless of which is true, however, the decision-making and overall direction and evaluation of the success of the project all rest on the shoulders of the sponsor.

Third, the decision on whether to proceed with the project happens during this initial phase. Costs and benefits are analyzed at a broad level, and the impact on the organization's stakeholders—employees, customers, shareholders—and how the project relates to the long-term strategy for the company are considered during this early phase. These considerations may appear to be more subjective than objective, but great projects start with data and an analysis of the impact a project will have before moving forward with the next phases.

Taking the necessary time to work through the conceptual basis for the project and the initiating data set, timeline, and goals is paramount to the success of the project. The OBM practitioner may take on one or more roles, such as SME, facilitator, or even a project manager leading the team through the phases.

Phase 2. Definition and Planning

Pathak (2020) described this phase well:

> A project management plan is developed comprehensively of individual plans for—cost, scope, duration, quality, communication, risk, and resources. Some of the important activities that mark this phase are making work-breakdown structure (WBS), development of schedule, milestone charts, GANTT charts, estimating and reserving resources, planning dates and modes of communication with stakeholders based on milestones, deadlines, and important deliveries. A plan for managing identified and unidentified risks is determined as this may affect aspects of a project later. Risk management planning includes risk identification and analysis, risk mitigation approaches, and risk response planning.

There are several tools to support the project manager such as GANTT charts. One key tool mentioned before is a project charter. Too often the project team is launched without a charter, and although we will later cover common pitfalls of project management, a lack of a clear timeline, support, and accountability are the results of poor project management. An way to avoid these pitfalls is to develop a project charter. In brief, a project charter includes requirements for the project, the business needs, a summary of the schedule, assumptions and constraints, and the business case, including return on investment (Brown, 2005). From an OBM perspective, the project team uses the data incorporated in the charter to make decisions, and the data provided supports both the initial phase and the phases that follow.

The OBM practitioner can take great aim at the definition and planning of the project. Pinpointing becomes a key technique in this phase—pinpointing both specific behaviors the project requires and who must perform them, the accomplishments employees should experience, and the desired business outcomes. Additionally, data-tracking processes should be defined in this phase. Data was used in the first phase, but data tracking for the level of detail the project team will need to truly evaluate the work needs to be in place, tested for accuracy, and positioned from a process standpoint.

Phase 3. Launch and Execution

With the senior management team on board, the project sponsor leading the charge, and the team in place with a project charter and details of the work ahead, you're ready to launch and implement the project. For the OBM practitioner, this step is important in the behavior-results improvement effort as **the "rubber is meeting the road."** With data tracking in place, the team engaged, and the details planned out, management becomes the key variable here.

Pathak (2020) described this phase as follows:

> A project deliverable is developed and completed, adhering to a mapped-out plan. A lot of tasks during this phase capture project metrics through tasks like **status meetings and project status updates**, other status reports, human resource needs and performance reports. An important phase as it will help you understand **whether your project will be a success or failure**.

The following article was originally published in *Business Science Magazine* in September 2019 and is used with permission by the publisher.

Today, project managers are in multiple industries and at various levels in organizations, with a scope of work ranging from small to large-scale projects. One thing clearly differentiates a successful project manager from a mediocre one: they don't forget the M! Managing a project requires more than just looking at the work activity list, timelines, Gantt charts, Pareto analyses, and meetings. The project manager is in a prime position to collaborate with the people executing the project, or the position of managing others and creating a positive work environment for all. The challenge, of course, is that most project managers feel they are not in a position of authority. So how can project managers take on the managerial role in the project? What does that look like?

Management can be summed up by a core set of behaviors:

> ***Providing clear and concise direction.*** To get behavior started, people need clarity of direction. Who does what, by when, and what are the basic elements of giving people the direction they need to be successful?

Measuring and monitoring progress against a goal. Without data, it becomes a guessing game as to whether people are doing what you set out to be accomplished. The goals may be achieved, but were they achieved precisely as you intended them to be? Management requires knowing whether behavior occurred as expected.

Providing positive, ongoing, and constructive feedback consistently. The team is launched, and the project manager has a key role, to provide feedback to the team. Without feedback, more guessing occurs among all parties.

Problem-solving when things don't get done or aren't done as expected. Challenges occur during a project, and a scientific approach to solving problems will support successful implementation.

Diagnosing performance, taking a "don't blame the person first" stance. Project managers should attend to the environment of any situation to ensure optimal success for everyone. Behavior analysis teaches that behavior is influenced by the environment, so the individual performer is behaving because the environment is supporting that behavior. Don't blame the person first; look to the environment to diagnose performance.

Holding people accountable when things don't get done on time or as expected. A project has a time expectation, and various activities must get done. If expectations are not met, management requires talking to people about the situation and identifying why it didn't get done on time and to expectations. Don't avoid it, people need the feedback, coaching, and direction—that's accountability.

Celebrating successes, wins along the way, and the goals achieved. Best part of a management job is celebrating the achievements of others, at least in my opinion. Behavior followed by positive consequences is more likely to reinforce the behavior to occur in the future. Take the time to celebrate the achievements along the way.

There is a wealth of literature providing theory, techniques, and research on management behaviors that accelerate and sustain high performance. The core set of behaviors I'm describing is derived from such literature, particularly applied research in the field of OBM. The lack of "management" focus in project management is astounding. In my own experience, project managers excel at scoping the project, analyzing pitfalls, and sharing information about progress. However, few project managers I have observed excel in engaging with people throughout the project, managing expectations across stakeholders, diving deep into solving problems with people before assigning blame, and recognizing accomplishments along the way.

Phase 4. Performance and Control

For the OBM practitioner, this phase should come as no surprise. The performance and control phase align well with the seven dimensions of ABA, specifically the analytic dimension. This phase is all about monitoring performance, managing the project per plan, and evaluating along the way to determine whether any modifications are needed, always based on data. For the OBM practitioner, the performance and control phase become where you would work side by side with managers and employees alike to monitor, manage, and maximize the performance the project is looking to achieve.

Pathak (2020) described this phase as follows:

> Occurring at the same time as the execution phase, this one mostly deals with **measuring the project performance and progression in accordance to the project plan**. Scope verification and control occur to **check and monitor for scope creep, change control to track and manage changes to project requirement**. Calculating key performance indicators for cost and time are done to measure the degree of variation, if any, and in which case corrective measures are determined and suggested to keep a project on track. **To prevent project failure, consider why projects are likely to fail and the ways to prevent failure.**

A few key points are worth mentioning from an OBM perspective, considering the words in bold. Without question, the OBM practitioner is focused on measuring the performance and progression. The key here is "in accordance to the project plan." This component is all about the integrity of the plan and ensuring we stick to the plan as much as possible. However, deviations can and should occur with agreement from key stakeholders. One element to monitor consistently is *scope creep*, which means something is beyond the project plan—resulting in additional costs, resources, and so on—and may not support achieving the goal of the project.

Lastly, considering why projects fail is important, and what the OBM practitioner can do is facilitate a discussion about the learning history of the project team and the organization. Past projects can support current and future projects via learning from the past regarding what worked and what didn't work.

Phase 5. Project Close, Move to Day-to-Day Operations

From an OBM perspective, the project close phase is an important phase for several reasons. First, it's a time to celebrate with the team, employees, and the senior management team. Success should not go unnoticed or unrecognized. Second, data is available to show the work to the world, based on a presumably positive impact. Finally, the project closes, leading to a door into the day-to-day operations. This door is about sustainability, or *maintenance* as referred to in ABA. Sustaining the impact made, the methods in which the results were achieved, and the long-term impact to all stakeholders. The OBM practitioner must establish a means for sustaining the elements of the project (behaviors, results, and resources to achieve them).

Pathak (2020) described this phase as follows:

> *A project is formally closed. It includes a series of important tasks such as delivering the product, relieving resources, reward and recognition to the team members and formal termination of contractors in case they were employed on the project.*

Project closure is not for the faint at heart. Special attention to the day-to-day operations to sustain the work. We recommend evaluating the policies and procedures of three business areas: (a) business planning and budgeting, (b) human resources, and (c) training and development. With these three business areas, the OBM practitioner can work with mangers to ensure policies and procedures include the pinpointing behaviors and results, and the necessary processes to enable them.

Pitfalls of Project Management

Photo by Christina Morillo from Pexels

With the five phases of a project now in your learning history, you're ready to better learn why projects can fail. This list is not exhaustive by any means, and you should engage with your stakeholders to learn from their histories as well. By taking these potential pitfalls into consideration, however, you may save yourself time, effort, money, and resources. More importantly, you might altogether avoid a failed project. Below are common pitfalls of project management:

> ***No pilot.*** During the early phases of a project, you may find pressure from the management team or senior executives to go full scale, organization-wide right away. In short, if you can avoid doing so, don't go full scale until you have a proof of concept—a *pilot* in other words. A pilot is a small subset of the organization. It is one department, one team, or even one employee. Testing the project regarding the behaviors, results, and specific solutions you're looking to implement (e.g., new technology, new procedure, new product). A pilot is an asset to organization-wide implementation. With a pilot, you not only learn a great deal but also establish proof of concept.

> ***No data.*** Hopefully, this will never happen to you given your OBM experience already. Data is your guide. However, some projects are

implemented with no data. The upfront data helped to get the project initiated, but the project was implemented with no further data to guide the implementation. Avoid this at all costs. Gather data along the way, on both the behaviors and the results; even sampling is better than no data.

No clear timeline. With the project in hand, and a project plan developed, you will hopefully not experience not having a clear timeline. That said, many projects fail because the timeline is too vague, because there are no real tangible due dates for deliverables, and because, most importantly, the team is working on general timetables (this year) versus a specific date.

No support. What we mean by this is tangible support—funding, resources, technology, and time. The verbal rhetoric of supporting the project is important, but not enough on its own. The project team, and specifically the project manager (which may be the OBM practitioner), should be advocating for tangible support following Phase 1.

No communications. During any project, especially when employees or customers will face a significant change, communicate times three. There is no such thing as too much communication when the stakes are high, change is required, and people are mobilized to make things happen. Corporate memos, weekly newsletters, progress meetings, and recognition events are all ways to communicate with employees about the status and progress of the project.

No accountability. Accountability is typically seen as a negative. Therefore, it is avoided or directed inappropriately. Here, however, we want to emphasize accountability as both positive accountability (e.g., people did something right) and constructive accountability (e.g., cutting corners and compromising to make the project happen). The OBM practitioner, the project manager, and the project sponsor should be holding people accountable using progress review meetings, analyzing the collected data, and using the project timeline. Positive accountability should not be under-emphasized. Rather, we believe in a positive approach to change, and the acknowledgement of positive behaviors and outcomes is what positive accountability is all about.

LABEL THE FIVE PHASES OF A PROJECT

To be an OBM practitioner is to be an assessor, implementer, evaluator, a manager of people completing tasks and activities to achieve an outcome, and of course, a subject matter expert in behavior science. A skill set that supports the OBM practitioner is project management, and for many it is a skill developed over a great deal of time. In this worksheet, label the five phases of a project using the descriptions provided.

Phase 1. _____

A project is formally started, named, and defined at a broad level.

Phase 2. _____

A project management plan is developed.

Phase 3. _____

When the "rubber is meeting the road."

Phase 4. _____

Monitoring performance, managing the project per plan, and evaluating along the way if any modifications are needed, always based on data.

Phase 5. _____

Includes a series of important tasks, such as delivering the product, relieving resources, rewarding and recognizing the team members, and formally terminating contractors in cases where they were employed on the project.

IDENTIFY THE PITFALLS TO PROJECT MANAGEMENT AND THE SOLUTIONS TO AVOID THEM

This list is not exhaustive by any means, and you should engage with your stakeholders to learn from their histories as well. By taking these into consideration, you may save yourself time, effort, money, and resources, and more importantly, you might avoid a failed project altogether.

No _____

No _____

No _____

No _____

No _____

No _____

❑ Not testing the project regarding the behaviors, results, and specific solutions you are looking to implement before full-scale implementation.

❑ Not gathering the information along the way, on the behaviors and results, or even sampling.

❑ Everything is too vague, no real tangible due dates exist for deliverables, and the team is working on a general timetable (this year) versus a specific date.

❑ A lack of funding, resources, technology, and time.

❑ There is no such thing as too much when the stakes are high, change is being required, and people are mobilized to make things happen

❑ Typically seen as a negative and therefore avoided or directed inappropriately.

CHANGE MANAGEMENT ESSENTIALS

Photo by Nothing Ahead from Pexels

When it comes to performance improvement in organizations, remember we're talking about change—change in the organization's core systems and processes, change in performance management protocols, change in the everyday behaviors to which people are accustomed. In some cases, the change can be in the very organizational values. Whatever the case, change requires care and attention to the impact on those who are being asked to change.

For the OBM practitioner, some knowledge of change management would be beneficial for three reasons: (a) the goals of OBM and change management are aligned, (b) both approaches involve interacting with human behavior, and (c) both are sought out by organizations, one more so than the other (guess which one?). For the Yellow Belt, we are including the following essentials of change management, and we will conclude with some final tips regarding changing performance. Here are the essentials we will cover:

1. A definition of change management and Kotter's eight key steps to effective change in organizations.
2. The three general levels where change management is applied
3. Change management and leadership
4. Managing change
5. Three phases of change management and how OBM fits in
6. The importance of the "sign-off"

A Definition of Change Management and Kotter's Eight Key Steps to Effective Change in Organizations

Change management is defined as "the application of a structured process and set of tools for leading the people side of change to achieve a desired business outcome" (Prosci, 2020). One of the more prolific authors in the area of change management in organizations is John Kotter, author of the book *Leading Change*.

Kotter (2012) described eight key steps to effective change in organizations. Below, I will review each one and provide an OBM perspective.

1. **Establish a sense of urgency.** Change requires a reason. Accordingly, either the lack of a clear reason for change or, more importantly, the lack of a time-bound need for change can lose the change effort before it even begins. From an OBM perspective, the sense of urgency becomes the ultimate antecedent for change. Urgency sets the tone for the "why" behind the change. Imagine a manager suggesting a change to a procedure but being shaky on the reason behind changing it or suggesting the change but saying "there's no rush to change this." This lack of urgency sends a clear signal of a lack of need, a lack of imminence, and a lack of potential reinforcement for making the change. In other words, to make change happen, a sense of urgency makes things happen fast!

2. **Create a guiding coalition**. Being on the same page about change exponentially accelerates the change. In life as in business, working with others to make change happen is best when everyone is working as a unit.

Creating a guiding coalition is all about a cohesive and unifying goal that brings people together to make change happen. The guiding coalition is a group of individuals who bring others together, influence others, and lead others with a vision and clear process through the change. From an OBM perspective, the guiding coalition of individuals should be viewed as a stimulus for change—the coalition represents the right antecedent for the change to be demonstrated. These individuals are typically SMEs, managers, and leaders, to use a broad sense of the term, and each of them is leading the change itself.

3. **Develop a vision and strategy**. For any change, the direction of the change regarding vision and strategy is critical to the change itself. With a clear visionary story and action behind the rhetoric, the people who need to engage in the change will have a sense of purpose. Kotter (2012) described six characteristics of a great vision statement: imaginable, desirable, feasible, focused, flexible, and communicable. From an OBM perspective, these characteristics of a vision can serve well in evaluating the behaviors associated with each. For example, for a vision statement to be imaginable, the people of the company must be able to vocalize how the vision could be realized in practice. Another example using the characteristic of focus would be observable with regard to goals, described desirable behavior, and of course, the level of priority based on the sense of urgency.

4. **Communicate the change vision**. What good is a vision if it cannot be communicated? In the realm of change management, there is no such thing as too much communication or over-communicating. From an OBM perspective, communicating the vision is a series of antecedents to prompt the desired behaviors. The communication itself can be evaluated regarding effectiveness. As Kotter (2012) described, the use of a story or metaphor, multiple media, simplicity, repetition, and modeling are all key variables of good communication. In addition, OBM practitioners can evaluate the impact of the communications related to the change by asking the people within the company if they can (a) recite the messaging of the change and (b) what impact the message had on them—Was it inspiring? Thought provoking? Worrisome?

5. **Empower employees for broad-based action**. Change can be accelerated by granting employees accountability and responsibility to make decisions, act, and offer support when implementing the change. From an OBM perspective, as a result of enabling employees, self-management, self-eval-

uation, and contact with reinforcers all come within the control of the employee. These elements are heavily researched in the fields of ABA and OBM as being supportive for effective change. This fact does not mean supervisors, managers, and executives don't play a role. Not only can these roles do the enabling, but the individuals serving in these roles can also provide the resources and positive consequences for the employees making such change happen.

6. **Generate short-term wins**. *Quick wins* are a set of activities yielding outcomes that are visible, valuable, and were low effort to achieve (Gavoni & Rodriguez, 2016). As Kotter (2012) described, generating quick wins helps to maintain belief, keeps the critics at bay, and refuels the momentum for change.

7. **Consolidate gains and produce more change**. With each success within a change effort comes the need for the organization to recognize those achievements, sustain them, and produce even more change. Kotter (2012) described how effectively implementing several small changes allows for tackling a larger change effort. From an OBM perspective, the goal is to achieve reinforcement throughout the change. Recognition, rewards, and continued behavior change will support continuous improvement and allow for more change efforts to be implemented.

8. **Anchor new approaches in the culture**. This step is about sustainability. The new approaches must be embedded into the day to day. Just like in project management, any change effort must be integrated into day-to-day business operations.

"The data are abundantly clear. The better we apply change management, the more likely we are to meet project objectives" (Prosci, 2020).

Three General Levels at Which Change Management Is Applied

1. **Individuals**: Enabling people to be successful in their jobs is critical in everyday business. When an individual is needed to make major changes in how they perform their work, change management can support the individual to accelerate their change versus hitting walls.

2. **A project**: Driving adoption and usage of the change toward a return on investment.

3. **The enterprise:** Strategic intent of change management is the focus, mitigate saturation and improve agility.

"Any level ultimately focuses on how to help employees embrace, adopt and utilize a change in their day-to-day work" (Prosci, 2020).

Change management and leadership.

We have discussed leadership and leadership behaviors during the White Belt, and now we are working through change management. The two topics come together as change management requires leadership, and leaders require change management.

> *"Cultural changes cannot happen without leadership, and efforts to change culture are the crucible in which leadership is developed."*
> (Quinn & Quinn, 2016)

From an OBM perspective, the world of work requires leadership. Managers manage change and make day-to-day decisions; however, leaders set the stage for change, set the vision with strong goals, and inspire people to pursue the vision and make the change happen. Managers can be leaders, as can employees, a board of advisors or directors, and the company executives. Typically, we begin with the executives as they are accountable to the highest degree for the organization. With executive management focusing on managing change efforts systematically and methodically, executives are, for all employees, modeling the behaviors of leadership during change. Executives' behavior is the antecedent for the behavior of leaders to support the change. The challenge for leaders is not to abandon a change effort following the communication of the change.

> **The announcement is the easy part**; it makes the manager look bold and decisive. **Implementation is more difficult**, because no matter how good and compelling the data, there will always be active and passive resistance, rationalizations, debates, and distractions—particularly when the changes require new ways of working or painful cuts. To get through this, managers must get their hands dirty, engage their teams to make choices, and sometimes confront recalcitrant colleagues—none of which can be delegated to subordinates or consultants. (Ashkenas & Khan, 2014)

Leaders understand there are typical reactions to change. For the OBM practitioner, having a clear understanding of these reactions is important as well given that the practitioner's role is to support behavior change toward achieving a bottom-line business outcome. In *It Happens*, Dr. Julie Smith (2002) described the three typical reactions to change—resistant, receptive, and resilience. Ultimately, the more resilient people are to change, the faster and more successful the change will be. Resistant people put up walls for change; receptive people will follow and do but only after others do or only to meet the minimum expectation. Resilient people make the change happen, help others through the change, and lead the change effort for the organization. Resilient people are the leaders of change management.

Smith (2002) provided a means for evaluating one's resilience to change. By answering six questions, you can begin to determine what you might need to change in order to be change resilient. Here are the six questions, which are useful for both the leader and the OBM practitioner working with the leader:

1. Am I proud of how I am handling the change?
2. Are my feelings about the change positive?
3. Are my thoughts and beliefs about the change positive?
4. Am I proud of my behaviors? (Consider whether you're doing things you feel good about, doing things you believe in, and doing things that help you move forward.)
5. Are the consequences to me encouraging my positive behavior?
6. Is my impact on others positive, especially people I care about?

Ideally, the answer is a resounding "YES!" to all six questions. Your feelings, your thoughts and beliefs, your behaviors, the consequences your will face, and your impact on others all influence your ability to be resilient.

Managing Change

Managing change is where the rubber meets the road. OBM practitioners strongly lean on their subject matter expertise during the implementation phase of change efforts due to being focused on the people side of change, their behaviors, and the environment that supports their work.

A model of change management by the organization Prosci (2020) is the ADKAR® model. ADKAR stands for the **a**wareness of the need for change, the **d**esire to participate and support the change, the **k**nowledge on how to change, the **a**bility to demonstrate new skills and behaviors, and the **r**einforcement to sustain the change. The model stems from good science in human performance, and the following table provides an illustration of how ABA and OBM relate to these elements of ADKAR. If interested in being formally trained in ADKAR and other change management tools, the OBM practitioner should investigate Prosci, the organization dedicated to the dissemination and education of change management professionals.

ADKAR®	ABA/OBM
Awareness of the need for change	• Need for change is a data-based decision: market trends, internal data. • Describing the need for change at all 3 levels: individual, team, and organization. • Expect to answer the "why" over and over again. It is important enough to repeat.
Desire to participate and support the change	• Individual motivation versus organizational motivation is not always the same. • Motivating Operation. • Desire to participate and support change needs to be "required" of management as part of their roles and responsibilities, without negating their own feelings/beliefs of the change. Desire comes by virtue of understanding the why.
Knowledge of how to change **A**bility to demonstrate new skills and behaviors	Apply Behavioral Skills Training – instruction, modeling, practice, and feedback. Repeat until fluency is achieved. Never assume knowledge on how to change.
Reinforcement to sustain the change	• Take a systems perspective: Top three – HR systems, daily operational processes, and financial systems such as budgets and forecasting.

With a preliminary knowledge base of ADKAR and how OBM "fits," you can work side by side with managers to support implementing change. ADKAR and Prosci are not the only change management models in the market, however, so we encourage OBM practitioners to stay up to date on the latest trends in change management.

The Three Phases of Change Management

Change management is strong with respect to structure and the process of implementing change. But one of the most consistent elements of change management is taking a phased approach. Different pieces of literature will have variations to the phases. For our purposes, we have defined three phases to change management for the OBM practitioner to utilize—(a) preparing for change, (b) managing change, and (c) reinforcing change. The phases are broken down broadly in the table below. OBM has a distinct "fit" in these three phases, they are illustrative under each phase.

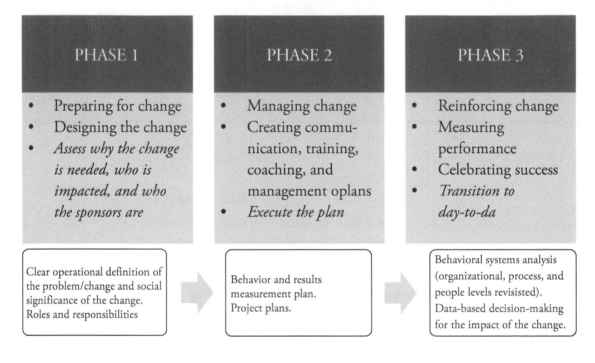

PHASE 1	PHASE 2	PHASE 3
• Preparing for change • Designing the change • *Assess why the change is needed, who is impacted, and who the sponsors are*	• Managing change • Creating communication, training, coaching, and management oplans • *Execute the plan*	• Reinforcing change • Measuring performance • Celebrating success • *Transition to day-to-da*
Clear operational definition of the problem/change and social significance of the change. Roles and responsibilities	Behavior and results measurement plan. Project plans.	Behavioral systems analysis (organizational, process, and people levels revisited). Data-based decision-making for the impact of the change.

The Importance of the "Sign-Off"

With this phased approach, there is one important element that cannot be over-stated—signoffs along the way from key stakeholders and the sponsor of the change must be achieved for each phase. A sign-off can be informal or formal, but history and experience suggest it should be formal. Once the work activity is complete in a phase, the OBM practitioner, the team of leaders stewarding the change, and the sponsor meet to review the phase accomplishments and sign-off that the organization is ready for the next phase. This sign-off goes merely a signature on a document, a verbal "yes," or even a head nod. The discussion should be a formal management review of the change. Did we achieve what we needed to achieve?

What has been the impact on others? Are we prepared for the next phase? What outstanding questions or barriers exist that need to be addressed? The OBM practitioner typically facilitates this discussion with the stakeholders of the change. The goal is to exhaust all possible points of concerns or issues before moving forward.

Permit me to share with you an example of the phases with sign-offs. Picture a large U.S.-based human service organization providing death care services—funerals, burials or cremations, and long-term care of the deceased individuals buried in cemeteries. The organization employs over 10,000 employees across more than 30 states. This organization worked with OBM consultants on a significant cultural change regarding how services were sold while maintaining high levels of customer satisfaction, improving employee retention and engagement, and increasing profitability for each location. The organization had been successful for decades. Competition was intensifying, and employee training and supervision were not heavily structured or organized but rather reliant on institutional knowledge by employees who were looking to retire. The OBM practitioners worked with the senior executives to define the vision of the culture change, defined "what good looked like" from both a business outcomes perspective and the behavioral lens at each location. Each location had a manager, supervisors supporting teams of salespeople, admin support personnel, and location service reps (i.e., cemetery crews).

Phase 1 and Phase 2 were signed off on by the sponsor, the chief human resource officer, the senior executives (including the chief executive officer and executive vice president of strategy), and the team of human resource and operations professionals selected to implement the change. Prior to sign-off, the roles and responsibilities were defined between the sponsor, the OBM practitioner, and the team implementing the change. After sign-off, the team began preparing communications, policies and procedures, training material, and a "management kit" for supervisors and managers regarding their respective roles in the change. The kit included objectives, data collection protocols for the business KPIs to be tracked and the behaviors to track as well. The kit also included the implementation team's contact information, and a designated team member each manager would be in contact with to review progress along the way. The sign-off came once all materials and change protocols were designed, reviewed by stakeholders (including employees at a few locations), and reviewed by the sponsor in detail. Prior to the sign-off, a pilot at three locations was conducted. The pilot served the team well by allowing them to learn from the managers, supervisors, and employees of those locations, and the team's demonstration of the new policies, procedures, training, and follow-up coaching to the managers was successful in improving customer satisfaction, employee satisfaction, and profitability.

Phase 3 began with a full-scale launch across the organization. Communications were sent to all employees by the executive team. Location management team meetings were launched to further communicate the vision, plan for implementation at each location, and utilize the management kit for the team to not only provide ongoing coaching and feedback, but also review progress based on the KPIs each week. The OBM practitioner worked with the sponsor to review progress and implement systemic improvements for long-term success, such as hiring and onboarding processes, leadership development for future managers, and a business planning process to include the KPIs used during the change. After over 18 months, the organization sustained significant gains—employee retention was at an all-time high, customer satisfaction improved for each location, and profitability was higher than ever.

The approach to this cultural change was structured, organized, and scientific. The OBM practitioner was able to replicate the successes from one location to another, systematically implement the processes designed, and use data to guide the decisions with the implementation team.

I hope this example helps to solidify the material we covered on change management and how OBM fits in. There is some great material on change management, books, peer-reviewed journals, and blogs by professionals in the field.

A Checklist for Managing Change

To support OBM practitioners, the following checklist is provided as a tool to use with your colleagues and clients. Implementing change is exhilarating work—difficult but exciting. Each phase in a change effort is important to ensure short- and long-term success. When you're an OBM practitioner, your differentiator is the science of human behavior. But tools and techniques from other disciplines provide a framework and structure to bring the science of OBM to the world of work. In addition, change management and project management are skill sets with a great deal of science behind them as well, from fields such as industrial engineering, industrial/organizational psychology, human resources, and business.

Phase	Checks
Preparing for Change	❑ *Defined why the change is happening* ❑ *Defined who is impacted and how they are impacted* ❑ *Listed the sponsor(s)—ultimately who is accountable* ❑ *Defined the key roles and responsibilities (responsible, accountable, consulted, informed)* ❑ *Sign-offs completed*
Managing Change	❑ *Established **a**wareness of the need for change* ❑ *Observed **d**esire to participate and support the change* ❑ *Provided **k**nowledge on how to change* ❑ *Observed **a**bility to demonstrate new skills and behaviors* ❑ *Planned **r**einforcement to sustain the change* ❑ *Listed the critical behaviors we need to see as part of this change and by whom* ❑ *Listed the business results we are striving to achieve as part of this change* ❑ *Sign-offs completed*
Reinforcing Change	❑ *Defined how we will celebrate the change efforts* ❑ *Defined how we will measure performance (the more detail here the better)* ❑ *Planned how will we transition to day-to-day operations, HR, and management systems* ❑ *Sign-offs completed*

LIST THE ESSENTIALS OF CHANGE MANAGEMENT

Change management is defined as "the application of a structured process and set of tools for leading the people side of change to achieve a desired business outcome" (Prosci, 2020). List the essentials of change management we covered, and add in any key take-aways or "a-has!" moments.

1. _____

2. _____

3. _____

4. _____

5. _____

6. _____

CONNECT PHASES IN CHANGE MANAGEMENT TO THEIR RESPECTIVE COMPONENTS

Change management is strong with respect to structure and the process of implementing change. One of the most consistent elements of change management is taking a phased approach. Different pieces of literature will have variations to the phases. For our purposes, we have defined three phases to change management for the OBM practitioner to utilize. Using this worksheet, match the phases in change management with the descriptions provided.

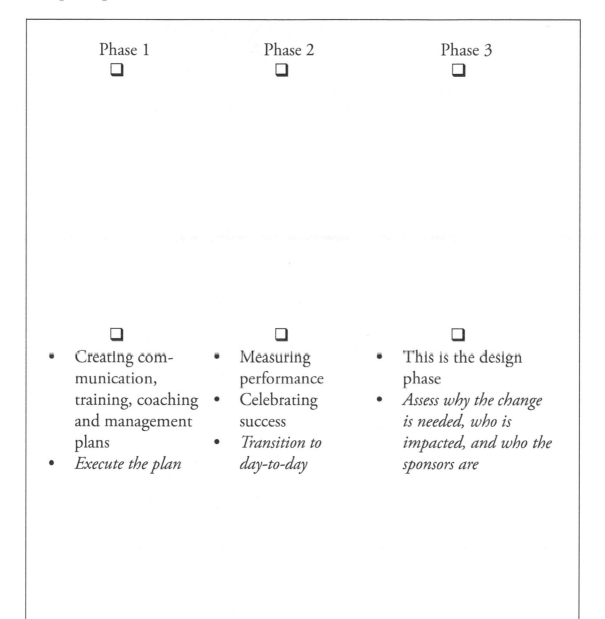

Phase 1 ❏   Phase 2 ❏   Phase 3 ❏

❏
- Creating communication, training, coaching and management plans
- *Execute the plan*

❏
- Measuring performance
- Celebrating success
- *Transition to day-to-day*

❏
- This is the design phase
- *Assess why the change is needed, who is impacted, and who the sponsors are*

OBM PRACTITIONER COMPETENCIES

Photo by Engin Akyurt from Pexels

The competencies of an OBM practitioner should inspire but not be seen as cast in stone. The following is provided by a group of OBM practitioners independently working on their own businesses but collectively supporting one another to further advance the field. With a collective set of experiences spanning over 20 years, the group created a set of competencies related to the practice of OBM. Over the course of a practitioner's career, these competencies can be developed through experiences, supervision, mentoring, and self-reflection. The practitioner analyzes their behavior against these competencies and the management of the competencies. The competencies are organized in four categories: content, analytical, process, and behavioral. A list of source materials is also provided as the basis for the list of competencies.

Content

Applied behavior analysis (ABA): The foundation of OBM is ABA, which includes a deep knowledge base of the concepts and principles of ABA, philosophy, measurement, experimental design, ethics, assessment, behavior change procedures, and the supervision/management of people.

Organizational behavior management: OBM practitioners have an array of focus areas, such as leadership, pay for performance, behavioral systems analysis, behavior-based safety, consumer behavior analysis, and more. The professional will develop skills in various OBM-specific areas, dependent on the member with which the intern is paired.

History of OBM: Just like other fields of practice, OBM has historical roots beyond ABA, such as industrial engineering and systems thinking. A good understanding of the history will support the OBM practitioner's practice and future activities, maintaining OBM as the core.

Business knowledge: A general understanding of how businesses operate to achieve desired goals is necessary for all OBM practitioners. The OBM practitioner should understand a client's organization from the perspective of how it generates revenue, who the customer base is, the products and services offered, and the supply chain of those products and services.

Economics and behavioral economics: A basic understanding of economics serves the OBM practitioner very well. Scarcity of resources, supply and demand, incentives, and purchasing power, to name a few, should be studied and understood by the OBM practitioner.

Learning systems: The OBM practitioner focused on learning and development would benefit from a strong knowledge base of talent and learning solutions when addressing human performance needs relative to business goals. Learning management systems, computer-based instructional aids, and adult learning theory can support the OBM practitioner's practice.

Technology knowledge: Knowledge of software solutions to consider when addressing performance improvement, specifically at a macro (systems) level for organizational effectiveness, will increase the efficiency and effectiveness of an OBM practitioner.

Sales and marketing: The major focus of OBM practice is service-oriented. An understanding of selling and marketing the services of an OBM practitioner and the products the OBM practitioner can develop (i.e., books, curriculum, training) supports the efforts of obtaining client-facing work. This premise is also true for practitioners working within a company as an internal consultant.

Analytical

Analysis: A core responsibility of the OBM practitioner is to analyze data. The ability to

gather, synthesize, and report and recommend actions based on data is critical for the practitioner.

Strategic thinking: Clients of OBM practitioners will be focused on the short- and long-term goals of their businesses, and in most cases, a client will have the ability to think strategically. The OBM practitioner should be able to identify opportunities to improve and set needed actions to allow the client to a gain competitive advantage for long-range goals. This focus is also true for the practitioner's own practice. The OBM practitioner should be thinking strategically of the businesses current versus future state and understanding how to analyze the landscape of the organization's competition, market need and demand, and direction.

Systemic thinking: The OBM practitioner takes a systems approach to performance improvement. This core competency should be developed early in the OBM practitioner's learning and then applied within every client engagement.

Process

Project management: Without question, the OBM practitioner will be managing projects, either their own internally for an organization or externally for their clients. Accordingly, planning, organizing, monitoring, and managing the work to be done by the practitioner themselves and, more than likely, others in support of a specific project is a set of skills to be developed and mastered by the OBM practitioner.

Change management: A field of practice and discipline unto itself, change management garners its reputation as the dealing with "emotional side of change." The OBM practitioner must garner skills in preparing, supporting, and taking actions to drive positive change in line with organizational goals.

Instructional design: The OBM practitioner should have a knowledge base of instructional design related to theories and models (e.g., ADDIE, adult learning theory, teaching and learning theories) and the ability to design methods of instruction and facilitate learning.

Facilitation and presentation: The OBM practitioner often finds themself facilitating meetings and training, presenting at industry and OBM conferences, and overall standing and delivering content to an audience. The skills garnered to perform such tasks is a competency that must be not only targeted but also trained to fluency.

Influencing: Influencing skills in the context of OBM practice is about demonstrating the expression of ideas with integrity, proposing well-thought-out scopes of work or plans to improve performance, and persuading others to make decisions based on data, research, and scientific principles.

Questioning: The OBM practitioner will get involved in sales, assessments, and coaching-related activities as part of their work. Across these and other activities, the effective use of questions and deriving actions from the responses to those questions (i.e., scope of work, recommendations, coaching actions) is a set of skills the practitioner needs to foster over the course of their career.

Relationship-building and management: Establishing, defining, managing, and evolving the relationships with clients, peers, and team members is a critical set of skills to develop. The majority of the OBM practitioner's business will come from relationship-building management.

Behavioral

Results-oriented: The OBM practitioner focused on just behavior is missing the link to the business. Being results-oriented is a set of skills developed by the practitioner regarding aligning behaviors to accomplishments to business outcomes, analyzing trends in business outcomes, and then identifying behaviors that will positively impact those outcomes while paying constant attention to the connections. Being results-oriented is also related to managing projects to achieve short-term milestones, deliverables, and overall goals.

Communication: An OBM practitioner must be able to communicate clearly and concisely. The practitioner should include pertinent information and data in consumable ways for the reader. In a person-to-person context, communication should yield desirable outcomes, including via conflict resolution, problem-solving, and performance feedback.

Behavioral flexibility: The behavior analyst adapts based on data, and the OBM practitioner must have these skills as well. Modifying the plans based on data and the proper stakeholder is part of the OBM practice. In addition, behavioral flexibility accounts for working with other professions that are not working from an OBM foundation. HR professionals, organizational design and development experts, I/O psychologists, and general business practitioners will be part of the OBM practitioner's circle of peers; having flexibility in how the OBM practitioner approaches performance improvement, without losing the integrity of OBM.

Objectivity: Applying data-based, bias-free approaches to various contexts is an important competency. The OBM practitioner needs to maintain objectivity in the face of a client who has biases and subjective reasoning, the peer who is operating from a different philosophy, or the boss who has a set of contingencies working against objective logic.

Working with ambiguity: In some cases, the goal, process, and/or roles and responsibilities to execute work are unclear. The OBM practitioner must manage such situations and focus on problem-solving and working with others to resolve the context to achieve a positive outcome.

Ethics and guiding principles: A solid base of ethics and guiding principles of the practice of OBM is pertinent to maintain the integrity of the field. OBM practitioners derive ethical codes of conduct or guidelines from various sources. At a minimum, the practitioner should have such guidelines as part of their practice, with constant vigilance of self-monitoring, evaluation, and supervision for situations that challenge the practitioner.

These competencies should be routinely evaluated by the OBM practitioner, a sort of self-evaluation of the skills and abilities that support the efficacy of your practice.

CLASSIFY THE CONSULTING COMPETENCIES

Over the course of a practitioner's career, these competencies are developed through a set of experiences, supervision and mentoring, self-reflection, and analysis and management of these competencies. Classify each of the consulting competencies by matching the competencies to the category to which they relate.

Applied behavior analysis, organizational behavior management, history of OBM, business knowledge, economics and behavioral economics, learning systems, technology knowledge, and sales and marketing

❑ PROCESS

Analysis, strategic thinking, and systems thinking

❑ BEHAVIORAL ATTRIBUTES

Project management, change management, instructional design, facilitation and presentation, influencing, questioning, and relationship-building and management

❑ CONTENT

Results-oriented, communication, behavioral flexibility, objectivity, working with ambiguity, ethics and guiding principles

❑ ANALYTICAL

MY NOTES

THE FIVE P'S OF AN OBM PROJECT EXPANDED

Photographer Negative Space, Man Walking on Sidewalk Near People Standing and Sitting Beside Curtain-wall Building, Retrieved through Pexels, Uploaded at January 12, 2016

With the foundational knowledge in project management and change management, the OBM practitioner has a framework to organize and execute an OBM project. An existing series of organizational systems support the implementation of behavior change solutions (e.g., coaching and feedback) yet are often overlooked. In consideration of preparing OBM practitioners, let's start with a detailed review of five key systems the OBM practitioner should ensure is in every OBM project, affectionately referred to as the five P's (Rodriguez, 2018). For the purposes of this course, we have expanded on the five P's from the original literature.

Stakes in the Ground

A metaphor commonly used in the work place is "putting stakes in the ground." A "stake" can take various forms, such as a fact (we have a budget to stick to), a decision made prior to a discussion (we have four weeks to implement the next procedure), a foundational type of statement (the sky is blue), or a time stamp for the audience (the meeting is to discuss what we are doing this week not next year). Stakes in the ground help set the stage for things to happen and do not derail people's attention from focusing on critical items.

Let's establish some OBM stakes in the ground:

1. Always remember an OBM project is the application of applied behavior analysis in business settings. The science of behavior has an intentional goal: to positively influence change, any change, in workplace performance.

2. The OBM project can be a small- or large-scale change effort from procedural changes on daily activities to a major merger/acquisition.

3. The OBM project can improve a process affecting multiple departments (e.g., HR, Operations, Sales, Marketing) or a daily practice (e.g., proper lifting techniques).

4. OBM applies the scientific method to achieve tangible results, such as revenue/sales, quality, productivity, safety, and so on.

5. OBM is interdisciplinary. Behavior analysis is the foundation. Other fields—such as industrial engineering, industrial/organizational psychology, organizational design and development, and organizational behavior—have influenced both OBM and the world of business.

With those stakes in the ground, it's time to work through the five P's expanded from its original publishing (Rodriguez, 2018).

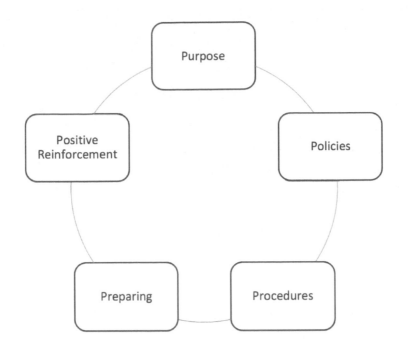

Purpose

Could you imagine going day-to-day to work without a clear purpose of what contribution you make to the customer, the company, or even your own profession? When an OBM project is set to launch, it must have a clear purpose. "The purpose of the project sets the tone, direction and overarching goal of the project. Without clarity in purpose, what the heck are we working towards" (Rodriguez, 2018). The purpose is clear when the following is true:

- There is a clear vision statement, an inspiring picture of what the change will look like at the end, the goals to achieve, and how success will be measured.

- The following questions can be answered by each and every employee, the CEO down to the hourly employee, and back up again: *Why are we doing this? Why now? Why didn't we do it last year? Why not wait until next year?* The "*why*" to a project should be answered by everyone.

- Success criteria is clear. Measuring progress related to the change is defined—the targeted business results, the value-adding behaviors, and how the implementation will be evaluated.

- Roles and responsibilities are spelled out. Change requires people to behave in ways to make things happen, and managers to manage the change. The roles and responsibilities of an OBM project are clear from the onset, including the role of the OBM practitioner.

Chavez (2019) described how the purpose of a project links to three keys to a project's success:

1. Investing in actively engaged executive sponsors
2. Avoiding scope creep
3. Maturing value delivery capabilities

Additionally, Chavez (2019) summarized the four principles and tips from the work by Antonio Nieto-Rodriguez's book *The Project Revolution—How to Succeed in a Project Driven World*. The four principles and tips are below:

1. Prioritize purpose
2. Formulate the purpose by asking why
3. Align the individuals
4. Ensure project leadership is embedded in purpose

The following quote by Chavez (2019) summarizes great perspective on the power of purpose: "Purpose elevates everything to the human level, beyond task. It is a key to differentiating project leadership from mere management. You need project management skills, but without purpose, you can't move into project leadership, which is about inspiration, engagement and energy."

In defining the purpose of the project, consider the following steps by Alexander (2020) as she describes how define the project scope:

1. Work with key stakeholders to define and create a scope statement by identifying what is within scope and out of scope. Collaborating with stakeholders helps to ensure essential things do not fall through the cracks.

2. Identify, document, and communicate assumptions. Assumptions are those elements that relate to the project that are assumed to be true for the duration of the project. Assumptions are necessary to provide an estimate of the cost and schedule to deliver the project's scope during the planning phase of a project.

3. Gain buy-in for the scope statement with the stakeholders who are most impacted to ensure everyone is on the same page.

Policies

Corporate policies are a staple of business. They set the tone for what is acceptable, what is not, and what minimum criteria is set as standard. The difficulty with corporate policies is in the execution. When people don't adhere to the policies, a behavior analyst would assess the situation as a lack of reinforcement for following the policy, and a lack of punishment for not following the policy. Policies without effective consequence management are simply academic exercises documenting the "should be" world of a business with no real teeth.

OBM projects should be supported by corporate policies, and OBM projects can support implementing corporate policies. Attendance policies, safety and health standards, and even ethical codes of conduct are all policies intended to support performance management of the employees within the company. In some cases, new policies need to be written to ensure a successful OBM project. There are several ways this may look in practice:

- **Policy starts with the top.** Existing policies are reviewed and modified as needed, new policies are written, and executives speak to the policy—providing clear links between policy and the OBM project.

- **Policy guides decision-making**. An OBM project looks to make decision-making clear and data-based. One set of data is the very policies that are intended to govern decision-making.

- **Policy enforces consequences**. No surprises: if you follow the policy, positive reinforcement can be the focus, but if you don't follow the policy, negative consequences will follow. This structure helps the OBM project maintain its course to making a positive difference. Loosely executed policies don't make for a successful OBM project.

- **Policy governs new behavior**. Change in business results requires new behavior; thus, policies set new rules to follow at a minimum.

Starting at the top

Photo by Marily Torres from Pexels

No matter the scenario, whether it is an individual starting a new business, a CEO taking over a Fortune 100 company, or anything between the two, the top manager has a responsibility and obligation to the organization to set the tone of what is acceptable and not acceptable practices by all who represent the company. Policies therefore are the tone set by the top. They describe in writing the intricate "ins" and "outs" of conduct to which the organization is holding itself accountable. The OBM practitioner can support the top executives in clearly and precisely crafting policies to avoid any misinterpretation.

Consider the following scenario:

> An executive wants to set a new policy regarding employee attendance, marking a significant change from past policy allowing employees to contact their supervisor within 24 hours before taking a paid day off to requiring 30 business days advance notice and approval before taking paid time off. The behavioral change required is not just the employees requesting their paid time off, but the supervisors and managers approving the time off and

adjusting work schedules to account for employees not working once approved. The executives clearly see the benefit for such a change, namely better planning of staff resources.

In this scenario, the OBM practitioner can support the executives by operationally defining the behaviors of both personnel seeking approval for paid time off, and the supervisors and management team members' approval process and resource allocation practices. By operationally defining the behaviors, the organization will have a clear policy, no room for interpretation, and clear accountability regarding the desired process to follow.

Another level of support the OBM practitioner offers is in the communication and surety of "knowledge" or "understanding" of the new policy. One-time communication is not sufficient to ensure knowledge or understanding of a new policy. The OBM practitioner can provide guidance and leadership regarding disseminating of the policy, measuring the dissemination, and obtaining the information. Measures could include a successful distribution process, number of signatures obtained, number of discussions held with personnel, and number of concerns raised and addressed by personnel. These measures and others can be the differentiator between a successful launch of a new policy and a failed one.

Decision-making

A policy is a staple of business practice, and a critical component to policy-making is decision-making. A policy helps managers make decisions, or at least that's the very premise of a policy. One key element to a policy is to have an official owner of the policy, a steward of the decision-making of the policy. How the policy is executed and how people are held accountable to the policy requires leadership, an understanding of how issues are raised and decisions made with regard to the policy itself. One bad decision can make a mockery of the policy, making it obsolete from effective organizational management. To avoid such a mistake in corporate governance, you need a governor for the policy.

The OBM practitioner offers a unique perspective on decision making—namely an analysis of behavior and the consequences that affect the long-term performance. The ABC analysis is a key tool to evaluating decisions. Starting with the behavior, the operationally defined behavior versus the undesired behavior helps the decision-maker start with an objective lens on the situation. The antecedents are then identified as to what initially triggered the undesired behavior and what antecedents should have been present to trigger the desired "policy-following" behaviors.

Then the OBM practitioner looks to the consequences, both for the undesired and desired behavior. This action may seem "simple" or like common sense to the OBM practitioner, but experience suggests the action is not common practice. The OBM practitioner may fall victim to the trap of "going native" following organizational practices of blaming the employee or seeking a quick solution, such as immediate termination. But the OBM practitioner can avoid going native by remaining objective, staying focused on the application of the science, and identifying the course of action that will support reinforcing the policy and holding the "right" people accountable for the "right" reasons, which isn't always clear.

Consider this scenario:

> A chemical company with over 10,000 employees worldwide has a corporate policy around safety. The policy includes the company's values around safety, "safety first," and a list of standards for procedural safety, such as confined-space entry, electrical safety, and the use of personal protective equipment. One day, a group of employees violated a policy, circumventing a standard procedure for safety and initiating a job without the proper permits or safety equipment. How did this happen? At first glance, all the employees involved would be deemed as violating the policy and would be immediately terminated. However, where was the supervisor? Where was the safety professional who signs off on permits? Why didn't any of the employees follow the proper policy/procedures? Has this happened before?

Given the above scenario, there are questions that need answering. Because these questions actually have no answers, the OBM practitioner best serves the organization by helping work through these questions as they are the antecedent situations that either were not present or were not consistent with prior situations. Via an ABC analysis, we could truly identify the causal factors for why this happened.

The result of the above scenario ended with identifying three causal factors:

1. The employees were only in their first few days at work and had not completed their training—an error in administration of allowing employees to work prior to fulfilling such a requirement.

2. The safety professional was signing off on multiple work permits and had not reached that particular job in time—an issue with resource staffing.

3. The job itself was scheduled the morning of the job versus coordinated with the weekly schedule and thus not appropriately scheduled or coordinated across the organization—an issue of communication and proper planning for day-of work.

This scenario did lead to the employees being given an official warning; the management team members were also given a formal warning for a lack of managerial oversight. Improvements were also made in the planning and scheduling of day-of work. The ABC analysis helped to deconstruct what happened, how it happened, and the consequences to avoid it happening again.

Consequences

When it comes to a corporate policy, one typically thinks of negative consequences for not adhering to the policy. Disciplinary action, termination, and even legal action can be taken by companies against an employee for violating a corporate policy. These policies have "teeth" is a common expression, and it's not just rhetoric; it's behavior. To issue disciplinary actions, to terminate someone, and to make the decision to take legal action require thought, stakeholder input, and decision-making by management team members, in some cases at the highest levels.

But what happens when there is no "teeth" behind the policy. Think about a safety policy that does not protect employees or consumers, a health policy that does not protect your medical records, or the sexual harassment that leads to no action against the harasser. In behavioral science, punishment and negative reinforcement are powerful consequences to stop undesirable behavior. Understanding the power of punishment and negative reinforcement, the OBM practitioner offers a unique contribution to the world of business and the "teeth" a corporate policy should have.

Managing the use of consequences related to corporate policies is an important element to the whole five P's model. Policies should be evaluated throughout the year in regard to adherence, violations, the very consequences themselves, and the impact these consequences had on employees, consumers, and the greater society. An OBM practitioner should support the implementation of policies with systems for governance (roles and responsibilities), measurement systems, and reporting systems to upper management.

Procedures

Procedures are where the rubber meets the road. Every day, people behave to make work happen. Behind the behavior there are expected steps to follow (hopefully). These steps are what make up a procedure. Fundamentally, an OBM project includes written procedures to achieve the desired behavior and results. *You know you are doing an OBM project when the following is true:*

- The procedures are linked to a policy. There is no guessing. The procedure reinforces the policies; thus, the desired behavior occurs, as do the results.

- Implementing procedures includes the following:

    o Engagement among the people who do the work
    o Written job aides linked to the procedure, such as a one-page quick reference guide
    o A detailed, no kidding, every step and decision point, multi-page procedure is written by the very people doing the work and an SME
    o A process flow map, illustrating the sequence of steps, who does what when, and the outcome linked to the steps

- Procedures are intended to influence behavior; thus, performance measures are in place to evaluate successful compliance to the procedures.

Preparing

Every change project looks to ensure people are prepared for the change. What this translates to is work before the change is implemented, and the larger the scale of the change, the more preparation that goes into supporting people for the change. *You know you are doing an OBM project when the following is true:*

- Communications are constant and consistent. Organizations are served well when implementing an OBM project that includes various communication vehicles, such as kick-off meetings, townhalls, ongoing stewardship meetings, and ongoing communications about progress.

- Training is targeted, focusing on skill knowledge and acquisition, and transfer of training to the job. The OBM practitioner makes great use of instructional design principles, behavioral skills training, and work-to-fluent performance.

- Materials are designed to help people on the job. From communication materials (brochures) to specific job aides (e.g., checklists), all materials help prepare people to perform the job. Again, the OBM practitioner should design such materials before implementation.

- Technology today is abundant and necessary to drive performance. The OBM practitioner looks to utilize technology (hardware, software, machinery) to maximize performance and evaluate whether technology hinders performance.

Positive Reinforcement

The use of positive reinforcement (R+) is fundamental in an OBM project. We won't get into the science and history of R+ here, but for the OBM practitioner, there should be no surprise of its positioning in the framework. Performance improvement requires positive reinforcement. That's a bold statement to make, but I'm sticking to it. This statement goes beyond the old carrot versus stick way of thinking. Positive reinforcement is a science-based approach to making a positive difference in people's lives at work. *You know you are doing an OBM project when you can answer these questions:*

- Are we supporting people throughout the change, providing positive reinforcement for problem-solving, raising issues, and helping one another during the change?
- How is performance being monitored to ensure we're making data-based decisions and reinforcing such decision-making?
- What happens when we see desired behaviors and the outcomes of the behaviors? Do we recognize them? Reward them?
- How immediate versus delayed is reinforcement?
- How consistent and predictable is reinforcement?
- Do we see desired behavior improving or increasing at high steady rates?

The five P's of an OBM project provide a framework. There are tools and techniques to apply within each element of the framework, such as business case for change, writing techniques on policies and procedures, instructional design principles and the fundamentals of behavioral skills training, and of course, critical elements of positive reinforcement (measurement, preferences). I argue that, without a framework, the tools and techniques are useless; they may provide short-term solutions without long-term gains.

LIST THE 5 P'S OF AN OBM PROJECT

We began with the 5 P's of an OBM Project. List them here and use the space below, write down any takeaways or "ahas!" you may have experienced during the review.

The 5 P's of an OBM Project

1.

2.

3.

4.

5.

IDENTIFY WHICH OF THE 5 P'S IS BEING DESCRIBED IN THE SCENARIOS

Match the scenario to the appropriate P from the 5 P's.

1. PURPOSE

2. POLICIES

3. PROCEDURES

4. PREPARING

5. POSITIVE
REINFORCEMENT

❑ The business unit achieved their goals and per the OBM plan, each team member earned a significant bonus on their pay checks, and companywide recognition.

❑ Team members were trained formally by an expert facilitator and on the job until they reached fluency.

❑ Senior leaders present the state of the company, successes and failures, and the direction of the OBM project for the team to engage in.

❑ The OBM project team documented the steps employees should follow when tracking their data and reporting their data.

❑ The Human Resources team communicated a memo for the rules employees should follow related to attendance.

HOW TO EVALUATE SUCCESS USING THE SEVEN DIMENSIONS OF ABA APPLIED TO AN OBM PROJECT

Photo by Andrea Piacquadio from Pexels

n the field of ABA, practitioners are taught the seven dimensions written by Baer et al. (1968). These pioneers of the field provided the fundamental elements for the application of the science of human behavior, guiding modern practice and research. In the field of OBM, a sub-discipline of ABA, adopts these dimensions; however, rarely do we read or discuss these seven dimensions as applied in the workplace setting. After several rounds of brainstorming, reading, and writing on the subject of OBM (and of course, practicing with clients around the world), we have developed a summary of an OBM perspective on the original seven dimensions of ABA.

The purpose is simple—to highlight how the original seven dimensions are absolutely applicable to the world of work, with a twist! We want to engage the OBM practitioners and researchers of the world to see this link and make more of an effort to write about the connection between OBM and its theoretical foundations in behavior analysis. In addition, within the broader world of work, we want to highlight how our practice of making a positive difference in the workplace is guided by a high order of principles, namely these seven dimensions.

Dimension 1: Applied

The original text by Baer et al. (1968) helped shape the understanding that the science of ABA should first and foremost be applied, meaning working on problems of demonstrated social significance. In the world of work, practitioners and researchers alike should always ensure the work is applied as well, namely as targeted performance improvement of social significance to all stakeholders in the organization—customers, board of directors, executives, managers, and employees, of course. In short, applied is about having clarity on why the performance change is important.

Dimension 2: Behavioral

Dimension 2 should come as no surprise: it's behavior. ABA is dealing with measurable behavior. OBM practitioners and researchers are also looking to focus on behavior; however, in the context of the world of work, we look to ensure a clear link between behaviors and business results. Behavior of all involved in achieving the outcome is critical as well, meaning not just the performer of the behavior, but those who influence the performer's behavior. For example, if we want more sales people to cross-sell, the behaviors needed from their supervisors, the managers, and the executives become a focus to ensure complete alignment of behaviors to achieve the desired business results.

Dimension 3: Analytic

The dimension of ABA requiring demonstration of cause and effect of our work is the third dimension, analytic. When we're looking to make any improvement in behavior, our procedures should demonstrate the intended effect. In the world of work, OBM practitioners should be evaluating the solutions to improve behavior change and the business results associated with the behaviors. Throughout an OBM project, the practitioner, along with the client, should make data-based decisions using the information on both behavior and the targeted results.

Dimension 4: Technological

Our fourth dimension is about being technological. The goal here is to detail our solutions to the point where others can use our procedures to implement the same solution, with appropriate training and resources. In short, the goal of practicing with a lens on being technological is for our clients to have no long-term need for an OBM expert. Managers, supervisors, and employees can implement the very solutions we put in place to achieve performance improvement, as well as other OBM practitioners across the globe.

Dimension 5: Conceptually Systematic

The fifth dimension of being conceptually systematic is demonstrating a clear link between science and practice. Here, practitioners ensure solutions are derived from a specific theoretical basis and empirical evidence. Practitioners look to the research to guide the solutions, following thorough assessments and using strategies founded in science. For OBM practitioners, this guidance should be no different. Our analyses of areas such as organizational culture and targeted performance deficits require solutions based on sound research, and more so on the concepts of principles of behavior analysis. By taking such an approach, we are conceptually systematic in our practice toward making a positive difference at work.

Dimension 6: Effective

Effective is the sixth dimension of ABA, focusing the practitioner and researcher on showing a strong and socially important effect as a result of the solutions implemented. In the world of work, we would demonstrate effective practice of OBM

ORGANIZATIONAL BEHAVIOR MANAGEMENT

through return-on-investment, along with supportive employee and customer satisfaction. Being effective hits the bottom line of a business and must be measurable.

Dimension 7: Generality

Our final dimension is equally important: the dimension of generality. The focus of this dimension is on how solutions are designed from the beginning to be applied in new settings and continue after the solution has formally ended. What does this mean? In the workplace, if you implemented a solution in one department or one business unit, and the solution is successful, could you implement it in another? Will an employee or supervisor generalize their skills to other behaviors, in other contexts? In short, the OBM practitioner looks to design solutions in order to replicate success, creating generality of the solutions and, more importantly, of the positive impact.

List the 7 dimensions of ABA applied in an OBM context

We want to engage the OBM practitioners and researchers of the world to see this link and make more of an effort to write about the connection between OBM and our theoretical foundations in Behavior Analysis. In addition, to the broader world of work, we want to highlight how our practice of making a positive difference in the workplace is guided by a high order of principles, namely these 7 dimensions. List the 7 dimensions here and how you see them applied in a business setting.

Dimension 1. _____

Dimension 2. _____

Dimension 3. _____

Dimension 4. _____

Dimension 5. _____

Dimension 6. _____

Dimension 7. _____

Identify the dimension being described in the scenario

This list is not exhaustive by any means, and you should engage with your stakeholders to learn from their histories as well. By taking these into consideration, you may save yourself time, effort, money, and resources, and more importantly avoid a failed project all together.

Dimension _____

Dimension _____

Dimension _____

Dimension _____

Dimension _____

Dimension _____

Dimension _____

❑ The team evaluating our OBM project declared it a success, stating "your procedures demonstrated the intended effect."

❑ The solutions were described in such great detail the organization was able to replicate it all across the company, business unit by business unit.

❑ The Return on Investment was determined to be 6 to 1, an impressive impact.

❑ There was such a clear link between sales behaviors and the impact on revenue.

❑ The OBM project developed project management skills of the managers. Following the OBM project, managers were able to apply those skills to new projects.

❑ The OBM team documented the basis for the solutions, citing relevant case examples and theorems.

❑ The company's market share and stock price were plummeting, suggesting working on how to increase market share was of great social significance

FIVE DO'S AND THREE DON'TS

Pixabay, Person Marking Check on Opened Book, Retrieved
through Pexels, Uploaded at May 20, 2017

This chapter is dedicated to providing five do's and three don'ts to achieve a successful OBM performance improvement project, hoping it supports your pursuit in implementing OBM to any needs you may have. Note: This is my opinion only, not the field of OBM at large.

Do Have a Sponsor

In growing high-performing and long-lasting organizations, leadership often comes up. To achieve a successful OBM project, one main DO is to ensure you have a sponsor, a leader within the organization that supports you every step of the way. Sponsors of OBM projects provide direction, guidance, feedback, resources, and reinforcement for making the OBM project happen.

Don't Be a One-Person Team

Most OBM projects achieve success when a team is formed to make it happen. If you find yourself operating alone to make change happen, you'll more than likely get frustrated and/or demotivated by a lack of progress. Form a team, ensure the team represents the organization well and is committed to making the positive change happen.

Do Clearly Define the Behaviors and Results

There is an old adage—what gets measured gets done. Well, in the field of OBM, I would argue that what gets clearly defined gets accomplished. By defining specifically what behaviors you're looking for people to do consistently—with quality and without hesitation—you can successfully communicate and reinforce such an expectation. In addition, within the world of work, any behavior improvement to be achieved must have a business result (e.g., sales, safety, quality, customer satisfaction) to ultimately achieve. In short, behavior + results = performance. Focusing on one without the other is a recipe for disaster.

Don't Forget the Business Case

With any OBM project, there is a business result of interest. When addressing critical business needs—such as improving customer satisfaction, employee morale, sales and revenue, safety, quality, and process improvement—OBM projects have been proven to support all sorts of changes. One thing binds them together: a business case for change. We ultimately pursue such effort for a reason, whether it's to address low employee morale or even high turnover, customer complaints, reduced revenue, underperforming sales, injuries and, worse, fatalities. Whatever the case may be, one thing is clear—the business case needs to be front and center, so don't forget it.

Do an Assessment

OBM is a science-based approach; thus, any good science requires solid analysis of the current state. In short, identify what's happening before you make any changes, and evaluate why it's happening to ensure your solution to improve performance is the right one.

Do Keep Your Scope Focused

Many of us go to work and see opportunities around every corner. When designing an OBM project, one thing seems to be true—to achieve maximum success, the narrower the scope the better. As managers and leaders in organizations, we tend to want to tackle more than one project at a time. This undertaking not only overwhelms people across the organization, but also can overwhelm you. Focus on a key priority—a change that will bring visible positive impact and one that can be implemented without managing so many other projects.

Don't Rely on Training as the Solution

In many cases, training is determined as a need or as "the solution" to make positive changes. Indeed, training may be a solution, but I want to challenge the thinking of training being "the" solution. OBM is a science, so solutions should be based on the assessment. Training may be part of a bigger solution "package." Job aides, clarified expectations, new procedures, and a feedback system may also be part of the same "package." In short, don't rely on training as "the" solution; instead, ensure every solution is based on an assessment.

Do Measure, Monitor, and Reinforce

Some OBM projects can be achieved in a matter of weeks or months, such as clarifying a task and providing feedback, installing an upgrade to a software program, or providing refresher training on a skill already demonstrated by staff. Other OBM projects may take several months to over a year. Mergers and acquisitions, improving staff retention, and integrating systems and processes and new leadership development programs all require time, effort, and a bit of patience. Regardless of how long the project takes to achieve, the following activities should be part of any OBM project: measuring the behavior and results, monitoring progress by looking at the data, and reinforcing progress along the way toward achieving the goal.

List the 5 Do's and Don'ts

5 Do's and 3 Don't to achieve a successful OBM performance improvement project. List them here and using the space below, write down any takeaways or "ahas!" you may have experienced during the review.

1. _____

2. _____

3. _____

4. _____

5. _____

STRUCTURE TO AN OBM PROJECT

Breakingpic, White and Brown Wooden Box, Retrieved
through Pexels, Uploaded at May 16, 2015

There are only a few models or approaches to structuring an OBM project. Over the years, both clients and practitioners alike have strived to keep things simple, meaningful, and memorable when working toward identifying how to best approach OBM to implement change. The practice of Change Management has done a nice job organizing approaches to change, such as the ADKAR model for change (Hiatt, 2006). ADKAR stands for **a**wareness, **d**esire, **k**nowledge, **a**bility, and **r**einforcement.

There are several overlaps to an OBM approach to change in comparison to ADKAR, yet no one model has been universally accepted or applied by OBM practitioners beyond the scientific method or the works of Aubrey Daniels (1989) based on performance management. He provided a structure called a *performance improvement plan* (PIP), for which he illustrated six steps: (a) pinpoint the results and the behaviors, (b) develop a way to measure the result, (c) develop a way to give the performers feedback, (d) develop a reinforcement plan, (e) review the results periodically, and (f) develop an antecedent plan (Daniels, 1989, p. 217). In short, Daniels would present the approach as pinpoint, measure, feedback, and reinforcement.

In 2016, Dr. Daniel Sundberg, Shannon Biagi, and I took a different approach to providing a structure to implementing OBM and wrote about it in the four-volume book series titled *OBM Applied!* (Rodriguez et al., 2016). Our approach was to provide practitioners with an "ideal" structure for implementing OBM. We expressed how not all projects are implemented alike and stressed that the order of the structure should be flexible and adaptable. Our structure was as follows: project scope; behavior, results, and data tracking; performance diagnostics; OBM solution planning; engaging the doers; evaluating data; sustainability; and social validity. Some parallels exist between our approach and that of Daniels (1989), such as behavior, results, and data tracking. However, we decided to go further in teaching practitioners about how behavior analysis can be applied to business, hence adding the elements of performance diagnostics, sustainability, and social validity. We also added important aspects of establishing a business case for change, what we called *project scope*. Finally, using some great applied research from the field of OBM and ABA, we added engaging the doers and evaluating data. Now, these additions don't necessarily lack reinforcement from Daniels's approach; on the contrary, his excellence in teaching behavior analysis has evolved to include these elements in his most recent edition of *Performance Management* (Daniels & Bailey, 2014), which was an influence to my colleagues and I when writing *OBM Applied!*

I share this simply as a means of providing context to my proposed structure to an OBM project. Looking back, I believe the work we did structuring OBM projects within the *OBM Applied!* books was a solid and full framework for the OBM practitioner. However, the work is not necessarily "client friendly" as the language and robust content was intended for practitioners and not for public consumption. Additionally, we learned some novice OBM practitioners would get lost in the translation of our structure in practice when working with clients. This learning was important in the journey of instructing and coaching OBM practitioners—how to bring OBM to the masses and keep it simple, meaningful, and memorable. In writing the OBM Certification, I decided to take a step back, put myself in the shoes of my clients and those who would call themselves OBM practitioners, and answer the question once again—what is the structure of an OBM project? One night, I went for a walk, and I looked up at the stars and pondered this question over and over again. I kept repeating in my head the concepts and principles of behavior analysis and what I had learned in my early years as an OBM practitioner from the gurus of our field, including Aubrey Daniels himself. It dawned on me that, to keep things simple, for both clients and practitioners alike, I had to bring it back to the core of OBM projects. To keep it memorable, I am proposing a new acronym—S.T.A.R.S.©

OBM Projects—Look to the S.T.A.R.S.©

S.T.A.R.S.© stands for the very core elements of an OBM project. The elements will look and feel very familiar to the great works of many OBMers in the past. I propose this framework in honor of those who have worked so hard to bring OBM to the world at large. S.T.A.R.S.© stands for the OBMers' role in identifying **s**pecific behavior and results of interest; ensuring **t**racking systems are in place—data, data, data; ensuring **a**ntecedents are in place for desired behaviors; ensuring **r**einforcement (consequences) is in place for desired behaviors; and ensuring the organizational **s**ystems are in place to maintain the positive behaviors and results.

Now, let's walk through each element of S.T.A.R.S.© in much more detail.

Specific behavior and results of interest

When an OBMer is brought on to work on a performance improvement need, at this point, it should be of no surprise that the first focus area for the OBMer is to define the desired behavior(s) and the results of interest. There are two elements here worth highlighting, given that we've already deeply covered behavior and results.

"Specific" is the first element. Getting specific on the "right behaviors" and "right results" is a matter of working with all stakeholders in the change effort. From the front-line worker to the executive level, the "right" behaviors and results may not always be clear or consistently viewed. The OBMer takes careful steps in identifying, from all perspectives, the "right" behavior and results. As behavior analysts, we are prone to understanding and evaluating a definition of behavior that's operationally defined—it is so specific that it cannot be misinterpreted. The best way to ensure a specific definition of behaviors and results is to see the work in action. Now, in some cases, the very change being implemented is new to the organization, meaning it would be difficult to see the change in action. Simulations and experimentation come into play in such scenarios—or to use a simpler and more business-friendly directive, conduct a pilot study of the desired behaviors and targeted results. Without direct observation and analysis of the definitions, the test of specificity would be more guesswork than science. Avoid guessing; test your specificity.

"Of interest" is the second element worth discussing further. Whose interest matters? What happens if one stakeholder group's interest is vastly different than another's? Both questions are very important to figure out. When an OBMer is called to support an organization, typically the caller is from upper management or even executive levels of management. The interests of upper management and executives are typically strategic in nature, are usually long-term outcomes, and involve a group of individuals to be involved in the change effort—a department, a business unit, a region, and one division of the company, or the entire company. The scope is typically large, and the OBMer's role is to identify the interest and the reason behind it—the data, the business case, the strategic reason it matters to the company. Once these aspects are defined, the OBMer takes great care in keeping this interest at the forefront of all follow-up discussions with direct reports of the management team, from directors and managers to the very front-line staff doing the day-to-day work. The interest of the executive is vetted with these stakeholder groups. They may not all agree. They may not all understand. They may have different viewpoints as to what the data suggests the behavior and results should be. Regardless of all of the that, the OBMer plays a key role in defining the interest of the stakeholders—namely a scientist defining the problem and key variables of interest. At the end of the day, the business has a decision-maker on who makes the business case for the change. The decision-maker is going to typically be the executive who brought in the OBMer, and the OBMer's job is to provide all the data from all stakeholders to give the executive the information they need to make the final decision.

Tracking systems are in place—data, data, data

Believe it or not, most companies track data in some form or fashion. Typically, what gets tracked is what matters to the company. Revenue, customer information, employee information, hours worked, and costs are some basic data points most companies are already tracking. The challenge for the OBMer is ensuring tracking systems are in place to collect data on the specific behaviors identified.

Let's say the OBM project wants to track the number of workplace observations conducted by each staff member, focusing on safe work behaviors. A tracking system would need to be in place to gather the data of the observation itself being done, who did the observation, and the details of the observation. Additionally, what is the point of safe work observations? To increase safe behaviors and decrease unsafe behaviors that are related—thus, tracking the results of incidents would be important as well.

Another example is an organization interested in tracking specific customer service behaviors, such as resolving an issue within 24 hours. A tracking system would need to be in place to track the customer issue itself, who is resolving the issue, the time the issue was raised, the time the issue was resolved, and the verification of the resolution. Depending on the sophistication of the organization's systems, some of this information may already be tracked at such a detailed level.

The OBMer takes careful steps to ensure a tracking system is in place. Before creating a new system, an analysis of the current systems for data collection should be completed—*What is tracked? Who managers the data collection? What data reports are available, and who reviews them? What is missing in relation to the desired behaviors and results?* Once answers to these questions are determined, creating a data-tracking system is worked on with the end user, never in isolation. This approach is important because the end user is who will be managing the data-tracking system long before the OBMer is involved. The end user is not a person per se, but rather a role within the organization. This fact is also important—think about future job descriptions that will clearly state the responsibility of managing the data-tracking system for those desired behaviors and results. Looking at this future perspective will aid in your tracking system creation as well. Data systems today will most likely evolve over time with technology advancements and roles and responsibilities growing. Still, for the OBM project to be successful, the end user needs to be involved to support such future growth and evolution.

Antecedents are in place for desired behaviors

We have spoken at great length about performance diagnostics, such as the ABC analysis, the PDC, and behavioral systems analysis. As a result of these diagnostics, two things emerge—antecedents needed to encourage desired behaviors and reinforcement needed to sustain desired behaviors. Antecedents need to be in place first to initiate the behavior chain. Policies, procedures, job aides, training, technology, environmental infrastructure, and maybe even new personnel are all antecedent changes to be implemented prior to expecting desired behaviors to happen. The OBMer works with stakeholders to not only identify these antecedents, but also plan the implementation of them prior to the "go live" date of tracking the desired behaviors and results. In some cases, OBM projects take months to implement antecedents to avoid long-term issues. One way to accelerate change within an organization is to implement the change effort—more specifically, the antecedents—in a staggered manner across the company. Behavior analysts will recognize this language in regard to a multiple-baseline design. Such a design is super helpful for organizations to plan and see change along a continuum versus waiting for the entire organization to be "ready."

One final point about ensuring antecedents are in place for desired behaviors—do not underestimate them. A strong policy describing what will be rewarded and punished, followed by specific procedures on how the desired behaviors are to be demonstrated, and stellar training using the very principles of instructional design and behavior analysis (i.e., behavioral skills training) will surely provide a strong antecedent basis for positive behavior change. It's easy to neglect these antecedents as important because organizations do have a long history of ineffective policies, procedures, and training as examples. However, the antecedents are important for behavior change to occur, and history doesn't have to repeat itself.

Reinforcement (consequences) are in place for desired behaviors

Without reinforcement, behavior change will not survive. The OBMer works diligently with stakeholders, specifically the "consequence providers" from the management team, to secure reinforcement plans in place for desired behavior. From rewards and recognition to lateral and horizontal career progression, and even financial rewards such as salary increases and bonuses, reinforcement contingencies should be carefully planned and implemented throughout the OBM project and when the business results are achieved. The OBMer is aware of reinforcement preference assessments, and when identifying reinforcement options, a historical review of the organization's use of rewards and recognition will help identify what will and could work to encourage the desired behaviors. When reinforcement plans are done haphazardly, the wrong reinforcers are much more likely to be selected. Whether received too late, not deemed "fair" by the behavers, or not consistently implemented by managers, reinforcers can fail an OBM project via poor analysis up front and poor execution during the project.

The OBMer should use three rules when implementing reinforcement:

1. Ensure a plan for consistent execution is in place.
2. Vary the reinforcement between social and tangible reinforcers.
3. Apply reinforcement to all organizational levels—from the front-line workers to the executives.

Social recognition is very powerful, as are tangible reinforcers. Losing sight of this is a failure to recognize our own science.

Systems are in place to maintain the positive behaviors and results

We reviewed systems thinking and behavioral systems analysis. The OBMer looks to the horizon of the OBM project to ensure the desired behaviors and results are part of organization systems, such as the business strategic planning, hiring, training and development, and ongoing performance management. The organizational systems should be adapting the new behaviors and the relationship to the business results for long-term sustainability. Without such systems in place, the behaviors and results may not last. The OBMer works with functional leaders—such as HR, Finance, and Operations—to work through the systemic changes needed to sustain the positive improvements. Don't underestimate this important step.

S.T.A.R.S.© is a copyright of Bueno Ventures Management Services, Inc. 2021

Your OBM Project Plan

With the details around our S.T.A.R.S.© approach to OBM, creating your OBM project becomes an exercise of, dare I be cheesy, connecting the S.T.A.R.S. Work through the S.T.A.R.S. approach, identifying each element for an OBM project you either worked on in the past or want to work on. You may not have all the answers yet, but a starting point is worth the time. You can recreate this table as the intention is to document your project in a simple and meaningful way applying the S.T.A.R.S.© model.

CONNECT THE S.T.A.R.S.©	YOUR PROJECT
Specific behavior and results of interest	

Tracking system in place—
data, data, data

Antecedents in place for
desired behaviors

Reinforcement (consequences)
in place for desired behaviors

Systems in place to
maintain the positive.

S.T.A.R.S.© Are Backed by Science

Identifying the relevant applied research supporting your S.T.A.R.S.© is part of the role an OBMer plays. You want your OBM approach to performance improvement to be backed by solid concepts, principles, and research. This ideal is true for your analysis of the problem and for the very antecedents, reinforcement, and systems you're looking to put in place to encourage the desired behavior. Whether the concepts and principles have been applied to your specific behavior of interest, or whether the antecedents and consequences have basis in the same industry, behavior analysts look to maintain the science integrity. Thus, we link what we're doing back to the core of behavior analysis (concepts and principles) and applied research.

Now that you have identified your project, connecting the stars so to speak, look to the literature and identify the research or relevant concepts and principles that support your project. Remember an OBMer looks to all bodies of work—from ABA to business as well. Don't underestimate this step in your OBM work.

A solid business case for change has supporting data, and a change project should also have supporting data. Research is there for this purpose, and the literature in OBM is growing each year to support us practitioners.

The table below is intended to be used as a tool to document your projects research support.

CONNECT THE S.T.A.R.S.©	YOUR PROJECT'S RESEARCH SUPPORT
Specific behavior and results of interest	
Tracking system in place—data, data, data	
Antecedents in place for desired behaviors	
Reinforcement (consequences) in place for desired behaviors	
Systems in place to maintain the positive.	

Define S.T.A.R.S. OBM Projects – Look to the S.T.A.R.S.© - We reviewed the variables that make up the S.T.A.R.S. acronym, list them here.

S

T

A

R

S

Design an OBM project connecting the S.T.A.R.S.

Using the S.T.A.R.S. approach, identify a project worth tackling in your work place or from a past experience for sake of applying the method.

Connect the S.T.A.R.S.	Your Project
Specific Behavior and Results of interest	
Tracking system in place – data, data, data	
Antecedents in place for desired behaviors	
Reinforcement (Consequences) in place for desired behaviors	
Systems in place to maintain the positive.	

Identify the S.T.A.R.S. are backed by science

It is time to put your scientist hat to ensure validity in your project scope. What research did you pull from? What applied research exists to validate your approach? Write it down, keep a log, and moreover ensure you have done your due diligence to making your OBM project scientifically sound

Connect the S.T.A.R.S.	Your Project
Specific Behavior and Results of interest	
Tracking system in place – data, data, data	
Antecedents in place for desired behaviors	
Reinforcement (Consequences) in place for desired behaviors	
Systems in place to maintain the positive.	

10 WAYS OBMERS DO IT!

Photo by Christina Morillo from Pexels

I n 2016, I wrote a blog for Behavioral Science of the 21st century (*www.bsci21. org)* titled "Do It Like an OBMer—10 Ways OBMers Do It!" (Rodriguez, 2016). Forgive me in advance if the title offends; that was definitely not the intention. In fact, the idea here was simple—how do OBMers do what we do? With permission from the founder of the blog site, I'm sharing the post here as I believe these 10 ways remain true today.

OBMers do it through behaviors and results! It should come as no surprise to bSci21 readers that the No. 1 way OBMers do what we do is by having a focus on behaviors. OBM professionals offer a unique value proposition to organizations, namely the science of human behavior and how it can be used to make a positive change and achieve bottom-line business results.

OBMers do it with leaders! The OBM professional knows all too well the importance of the leader within the context of organizational change and improvement. The leaders provide the mission, vision, values, and supporting environmental factors that make or break performance. Thus, the OBM professional spends a lot of time coaching and consulting leaders because, without them, organizational change could come to a screeching halt.

OBMers do it with evidence-based approaches! Unlike other consultancies who use whatever flavor of the month or fad is hot right now, OBM practitioners are committed to utilizing evidence-based approaches in their work. This too should come as no surprise to bSci21 readers.

OBMers do it with data! Another fundamental way the OBM practitioner makes a difference in the world of business is through the use of data. Since the focus is on behaviors and results, it makes sense that the data we look to monitor and manage is both behaviors and results. There are means to determine when to measure behavior or results, or both. That subject is too much to cover in this article, but the OBM practitioner's focus on data is clearly a differentiator from other consultant types.

OBMers do it with many influencers! OBM is grounded in ABA and is clearly understood to be a sub-discipline of ABA. However, OBM is heavily influenced by other disciplines, which leads the OBM practitioner to have a multifaceted approach to meeting the needs of organizations around the globe. Disciplines such as instructional design, industrial and organizational psychology, organizational behavior, organizational development, systems analysis, and of course, behavior analysis have all played a role in the evolution of OBM as a science, field of practice, and body of literature for the OBM practitioner.

OBMers do it with a plan! Any OBM project, small or large, needs a solid plan. The OBM professional strives to ensure a plan is in place to design, implement, and evaluate the work. The plan can take many shapes and forms. However, one thing is clear—there must be a plan. Without a plan, you are destined for failure.

OBMers do it through shaping! Shaping is a common protocol used in ABA, and the OBM professional is served well to apply shaping in their behavior change efforts. A different way of looking at how shaping is applied by the OBM practitioner is from a common saying used by OBM professionals—"Start where the client is." Clients of OBM practitioners have various starting points. The clients may be well-versed in human behavior or naive, they may have implemented projects in the past with great success or be newly minted to the project world, and they may be a seasoned leader or transitioning into a leadership role for the first time in their career. By starting where the client is, the OBM practitioner can provide the right level of coaching and consultation to support the client's efforts in making a positive difference.

OBMers do it to make a difference! In the field of ABA, the focus is on making socially significant behavior changes. In OBM, the professional seeks to work on organizational needs significant for both the individuals within the organization and the individuals impacted by the organization. Whether focused on the front-line employee, the CEO, the consumers of the organization, and the shareholders investing in the company, the OBM practitioner must understand and apply a fundamental principle—we do what we do to make a difference in people's lives. Whether the OBM professional is providing training and development, coaching the CEO, or driving a specific performance improvement project to impact revenue, costs, productivity, quality, safety, or customer retention, the impact is what makes or breaks the work.

OBMers do it, and write about it! One of the most enjoyable aspects of being an OBM professional is learning from other OBM professionals. The *Journal of Organizational Behavior Management* has been a major source of inspiration and learning, and the journal is fundamentally a platform to build careers in the field. Since 1977, practitioners, researchers, and students in the field have written about their work, solidifying the previous points I mentioned above and other points I am sure I missed. Furthermore, the journal has evolved over the years, adding credibility to how we pursue our work and research to advance the science in parallel to how organizations work in the modern world.

OBMers do it with other OBMers! If you weren't aware, the field of OBM is supported by the OBM Network, a 400+ member special interest group of the Association for Behavior Analysis International (ABAI) and noted as the second largest group within ABAI. Over the years, the network has grown and continues to strive to grow the vitality and reach of OBM as a science, making a positive difference in the workplace. Many OBM professionals have collaborated through the years, supporting large research and applied projects. This unique aspect of being an OBM professional is a great value proposition for both the professionals and the consumers of our work who benefit from collaborations within a broader network of professionals.

THE OBM PROFESSIONAL (FROM OBM ENTREPRENEUR)

Photo by nappy from Pexels

Excerpts from Rodriguez, M., & Parks, N. (2019). *OBM entrepreneur: Launching your OBM practice* (1st ed.). 305 Publishing.

Relationship Management

You may have heard this before, but it's worth repeating: OBM is a people business. Cultivating relationships with clients, stakeholders, colleagues, and your broader network is essential. For the OBM Entrepreneur, we believe the vast majority of business will come from such relationships. Relationship management, from our standpoint, involves behaviors that set an OBM Entrepreneur apart from the competition. This list of behaviors for relationship management has evolved over several years of practice; however, we are encouraged that, over time, it will continue to evolve further.

Behaviors for relationship management for the OBM Entrepreneur are organized into four categories: establishing the relationship, defining the relationship, managing the relationship, and evolving the relationship (see figure below).

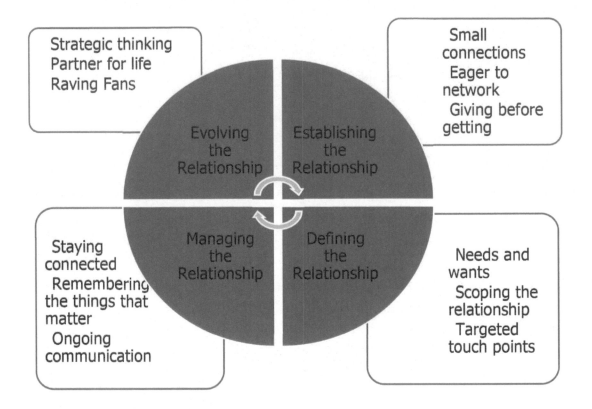

Each category consists of three critical behaviors that we have defined to support your relationship management efforts.

Establishing the relationship

When you're establishing relationships, it is important to demonstrate various interpersonal skills, body language, and a genuine interest. The challenge of these descriptors lies in the very vagueness of the descriptors themselves, necessitating definitive behaviors to focus on. For us, the following three behaviors support establishing a relationship.

First, begin with an introduction and identifying small connections with an individual that relate to yourself. Birthplace, career path, accomplishments, and industries you have worked in are just some of the many areas you can focus on to identify a small connection with another person. We are focused on the "small" not to minimize the nature of the connection, but rather to emphasize that the function of establishing a relationship is for a potential large connection, professionally speaking—client work, collaborations, and so on. At any given time, you can introduce yourself to 10 people and discover some connection you have with them. The purpose, professionally speaking, would be to identify potential clients or colleagues.

Second, we suggest not faking it to make it, but rather being genuinely eager to network with a purpose. How does one define genuine? If you have privately thought *I'd rather not network today* or have told others how you would rather be in front of computer instead of networking, then you will potentially visibly demonstrate a disingenuousness during your networking efforts. Some may be able to perform good acting skills while networking and not appear as if they would rather be somewhere else. Although you may still be able to network, get to know people, and even make small connections, for the OBM Entrepreneur, the goals of networking are to achieve some outcome—contacts and potential leads, for instance—not just act. With just networking itself as a goal, you may not yield the outcomes you, as an OBM Entrepreneur, are seeking when networking.

Third, establishing a relationship is much more about giving than getting. In practice, we refer to the notion of pairing yourself as a reinforcer. What this means in practice is executing on many opportunities to give others a positive experience from interacting with you. From the sales chapter, we referred to the Give to Get strategy, and in establishing relationships, it is all about giving—giving is a means of pairing yourself as a reinforcer.

Defining the relationship

Defining the relationship takes form after establishing one. Several interactions with others help to shape the relationship—whether it is a colleague, boss, client, or other relationship. Those interactions then ultimately lead to some defined relationship parameters. We want to break down defining relationships across the following three behaviors.

First, discuss and define various needs and wants as they relate to your professional practice. When defining the relationship, whether it is with a colleague or a client, we find it starts with knowing the needs and wants of the other party. Maybe the person needs your expertise, a book you have, an introduction to someone in your network, a proposal even, or of course, a more in-depth conversation about a possible performance improvement project. The nature of the relationship, professionally speaking, will be defined early on after you establish the relationship. Sometimes meeting people doesn't turn into a defined professional relationship at all. However, the OBM Entrepreneur should be purposeful in networking; therefore, over time, the relationship begins to get defined toward that purpose.

Second, scoping the relationship becomes a matter of understanding how the defined relationship will be executed, setting boundaries as needed, and ensuring clarity on roles and responsibilities. There is a lot to do in scoping the relationship, and it should not go unchecked. Who will do what? Are there limitations, boundaries, or conflicts that need resolving? Who else needs to be involved, and what is their role? This behavior may seem like project managing a relationship, and in a way, it is. Professionally speaking, once you have a defined relationship, clarity on the execution of the relationship helps further build a positive experience for each party.

Finally, we believe in targeted touch points at this phase. Contacting the relationship to finalize any parameters of the relationship, scope, and so on to ensure clarity and agreements are set is key. Think about implementing a project—how far are you willing to go in a project with uncertain expectations or unclear roles and responsibilities? If you go too long, it will drive everyone crazy. Relationships are much larger than a set project, of course, but those targeted touch points help to ensure everything goes smoothly.

Managing the relationship

Whether you're working with a boss, colleague, or client, and it's time to make the work visible, manage the relationship you have cultivated to that point, and ensure an ongoing positive experience with your relationship. Managing is about self-management of the relationship. Have you reached out to your client this week? When was the last time you reviewed progress on your work with your boss? Has it been a while since you and your colleague talked work over lunch? These relationships took time to cultivate, so don't lose sight of that. Actively manage the relationship. We want to break down managing the relationship across the following three behaviors.

First, staying connected is key. Active relationships should be part of your daily and weekly set of activities. Contact the relationship frequently to discuss those small connections as appropriate, and dig into the professional business at hand. Inactive relationships, again in the professional sense, should also have some maintained contact, but not as frequent—maybe quarterly or a few times a year. The objective is to maintain contact versus losing contacts.

Second, remember the things that matter. During the establishing relationship phase, you learned a lot about the other person. Ideally, you gained insight into the person's work, reinforcers, learning history, and existing work stressors. Pairing yourself as a reinforcer includes inquiring about those things that matter to the other person. From the person's family to work performance and career moves, knowing and remembering those things that matter to the other person, and bringing them up when it is most appropriate, further supports you as a reinforcer. Some of us forget, and behavior analysis would suggest forgetting occurs due to a lack of stimulus control. Our remedy to this forgetfulness is to take great notes about your relationship. From the small details to the large ones, write them down, and when you interact with the person, revisit those notes from time to time. Those notes can be the very stimulus you need to remember the things that matter.

Finally, managing the relationship requires ongoing communication. Depending on the nature of the relationship, "ongoing" will be defined by a frequency that supports versus hinders the relationship. If the relationship is part of an active project where you're working with the person daily, then ongoing communication can be daily or even weekly. If the relationship is a contact within your social media network, however, it is a strong relationship with great potential for future collaborations. Accordingly, a monthly or bi-monthly communication may be great to maintain the relationship and manage the possibilities. The point of managing the relationship is to ensure needs and wants, expectations, and stimulus control of your connection with the person are met. We can't stress this enough, but here is an illustration. One of the authors met a person in the early 2000s while at college. They stayed in touch year after year even though their paths only crossed one time in 10 years. In 2015, they communicated again as they have in the past and acquainted themselves with their professional happenings. At the end of three phone calls, they entered into a professional relationship, amounting to a six-figure contractual working relationship and, eventually, a success story of the work itself. We contend that, had they not maintained the relationship, the professional contract would more than likely not have occurred so many years later.

Evolving the relationship

At this point, you have great relationships that you have established, defined, and maintained. Professionally, these relationships are essential for the OBM Entrepreneur. In many cases, we have heard about and experienced relationships ourselves that have lasted decades, and each relationship has evolved into variations from the onset when it first was established—from acquaintances to colleagues and clients, to evolving to what we will refer to as partners and fans. To have a relationship that is a partner and/or fan is truly an exceptional experience and very much the result of both parties reinforcing a relationship that adds value, reinforces behavior that excels one another, and ultimately becomes a relationship worth evolving. We have summed up this phase into the demonstration of the following three behaviors for the OBM Entrepreneur.

First, demonstrate strategic thinking and action planning. Short-term, quick wins are critical for the OBM Entrepreneur. They demonstrate a level of effectiveness, focus, and immediate gains for everyone. However, to evolve a professional relationship requires OBM Entrepreneurs to work with their relationships toward a long-term plan. If you work inside a company, what multi-year strategic imperatives do you see as being needed in the organization? Striking up those conversations with key stakeholders could establish you as a strategist for long-term gains, all while using OBM as the vehicle to getting there. External OBM practitioners can do the very same. Working with the client, the OBM practitioner looks to identify long-term strategies, including those that will sustain the improvements made from the short-term strategies. For OBM Entrepreneurs leading their own businesses, this behavior of strategic thinking can be beneficial for evolving client relationships into long-term clients. Many OBM practitioners have worked with clients for multiple years, in some cases decades. The work evolves, the challenges may differ from one year to the next, and the relationship may change from an OBM project in one business unit to a global change management effort. But the need to demonstrate strategic thinking is both constant and critical, along with working collaboratively with your relationship to plan the action steps needed to turn strategic steps into a reality.

Second, evolving a relationship toward a partner for life is always something to strive for. We use the word "partner" in a business sense. Partners are in it with you—working toward the same goals, shared interests, and passion—and work with you to achieve those goals. Partner in the business sense means contractual partners, written agreements, and publicly endorsing your work together. The OBM Entrepreneur would do well with such partners, individuals looking to help achieve great things for the long run. If you have ever thought about writing a book or public speaking in front of large audiences, a partner could be a beneficial ally to help get you there. If you're looking to grow and scale your business, promote your services inside an organization, or even gain a promotion to an executive level, a partner can be your coach, mentor, and advocate toward achieving those goals. A partner is also a reciprocal relationship, meaning you are in the other person's corner as well, looking out for and helping your partner achieve goals. Evolving a relationship toward a partner for life is a great deal of behavior to engage in, and while this may sound more like a goal statement, we refer to it as a collection of behaviors to achieve the goal of partner for life.

Finally, reinforce your raving fans. Raving fans is not a new concept. A raving fan is someone who advocates for you and promotes you to others. Ken Blanchard and Sheldon Bowles's (1993/2004) book *Raving Fans* provides readers with examples and strategies for creating raving fans from their customer bases. Famous motivational speaker and business coach Tony Robbins (2019) also discusses creating raving fans, offering seven "commandments," as he calls them, for doing so:

1. Give more than you promote, reinforcing the Give to Get strategy; he even suggests giving 3:1 or 4:1 of "value over promoting your products and services."
2. Always leave your clients in a better place, supporting the need to understand their needs and goals.
3. Create unexpected surprises and bonuses, supporting the notion of positive experiences from your efforts and pairing yourself as a reinforcer.
4. Continually ask customers for their opinions.
5. Always reward your best clients, reinforcing your sales strategy of giving discounts; Robbins goes further to suggest giving your best clients "offers and value in addition to what your core clients are receiving."
6. Create a system encouraging everyone in your organization to meet your clients' needs, highlighting a systematic and planned approach to creating raving fans versus it being an accidental outcome.
7. Give back to "your clients, the industry and society as a whole," again reinforcing the Give to Get strategy but, in this case, doing so beyond the sales strategy.

The raving fan concept focuses on the client; however, we contend the suggestions for reinforcing your raving fans can be applied to colleagues, bosses, direct reports, distinguished professionals in your network, and of course, the clients receiving your services and products. Evolving your relationships to include raving fans requires acknowledging who they are and how you will reinforce their behavior of being your raving fans.

Consulting Roles and Responsibilities

Photo by edwin josé vega ramos from Pexels

For both internal and external OBM practitioners, the roles, and responsibilities of an OBM practitioner can be categorized into three areas, largely based on the work of Peter Block's (1999) Flawless Consulting: subject matter expert, project champion, and collaborator. These roles are critical to the success of the OBM practitioner, and for the entrepreneurial side of OBM, developing your own skills on how to leverage these roles can support your practice and business.

Subject matter experts (SMEs)

Being an SME is no small feat. When you walk into a room, the expectations are set—you know what you're talking about. In some cases, OBM practitioners feel the weight of being labeled as an SME. If you're an SME, people hang on every word you say. If you disagree with something others agree with, you can be the subject of a debate that may or may not work to your advantage. Finally, as an SME, you will give guidance to others. If successful, the SME label holds true. If failures from the guidance surface, you will be questioned, your integrity and credibility challenged.

Being an SME is critical for the OBM Entrepreneur; it allows you to set yourself apart from the competition. When you're truly an SME, you have a competitive edge. While building your expertise, be aware of your strengths and the areas of weakness in your knowledge and skills. OBM Entrepreneurs and practitioners must also decide what specifically they are experts on given their respective career history as OBM is a broad and varied field of practice. Consider your own history, and identify specifically in OBM where you have demonstrated success, value, and time in your practice. Various OBM Entrepreneurs and practitioners have demonstrated success and expertise in areas such as behavior-based safety, performance scorecards and pay-for-performance systems, process improvement, feedback systems, and preference assessments, as well as more industry-specific expertise (e.g., human services, banking, manufacturing) or performance challenge expertise (e.g., turnover, sales, safety). When performing the role of an SME, you may not actually be part of the project itself or doing any hands-on work. More than likely, you are engaging in a consulting capacity—providing input, feedback, advice, and direction. This role is important as your expertise is what people want.

Project champion

The OBM Entrepreneur and practitioner typically hold a key role and level of responsibility as project champions. Here, we're referring to the role you play in leading, sponsoring, and overseeing a project for a client, whether it's a paying client for your external practice or an internal client for the organization you work for. The work of a project champion is to ensure the success of the project and, ultimately, be accountable for the outcomes. For the OBM practitioner, we suggest this work is related to the seven dimensions of ABA. In addition, the project champion role may or may not be the architect of the project; however, given the nature of OBM practitioners having subject matter expertise, they have a great deal of influence on the project. We say "project" simply to suggest a start and end point, not in terms of time but rather from the standpoint of having an initial problem definition all the way to the result of an established criterion of success. The champion role is also responsible for ensuring that stakeholders are well-informed and buy into the OBM efforts, that feedback is gathered throughout the project, and that the integrity of the work is in check. This role is critical for the OBM Entrepreneur as selling and marketing work is one thing, but championing the work requires dedicated effort and shouldn't be left solely in the hands of those delivering the work.

Collaborator

What Peter Block (1999) referred to as a *pair-of-hands*, the collaborator role for the OBM Entrepreneur puts you in the seat right next to your colleagues, clients, and stakeholders. What are you doing that contributes to the project? Who are you working with to get things done? How are you helping get things done versus directing or just giving feedback? Collaborators have their hands in the work itself, putting their own fingerprints into the very work being delivered. Writing this book, for example, required all three authors to contribute text, feedback, illustrations, examples, and even ideas that got transferred into the book. Collaborators are doers, making things happen together for the ultimate achievement of the project goals.

Sustaining Success

Pixabay, View Of High Rise Buildings during Day Time, Retrieved through Pexels, Uploaded at January 20, 2017

Taking a macro view of the world of an OBM Entrepreneur, we need to know how to sustain our success. The careers of OBM practitioners are based on the very success stories of their practice. For the OBM Entrepreneur, it is the combination of the success of the practice and the financial stability of the venture, whether it be a salaried job with benefits or owning your own business and enjoying the rewards of profit distributions. But how does one sustain success? We, of course, are assuming you will indeed achieve success as a practitioner given the scientific nature of OBM. That said, it is important to call attention to some elements of sustaining success as an OBM practitioner, before looking at the entrepreneurial side.

For OBM practice to sustain success, we believe it is critical to focus on three key elements:

1. **The seven dimensions of ABA.** If your OBM efforts are aligned with the seven dimensions of ABA, you are already setting yourself up for success.

2. **Organizational systems.** In some cases, OBM endeavors take a micro look at performance, while the literature is clear that one must take a macro or systems view to ensure long-term gains. From HR processes to operations and finance, organizational systems must be clearly supporting the behavior-results work the OBM practitioner helped improve.

3. **The next strategic imperative.** While working with your clients, recognize opportunities to continue working with your existing clients on the next strategic imperative. OBM can be applied to improve multiple business needs. While working on one venture, look for more opportunities to work with your client. You can find yourself having a client for life, which supports sustaining your success as a practitioner while maintaining integrity in the science, and fading out when appropriate.

The ingredients to sustaining success as an entrepreneur are beyond the basics of OBM practice and may require you to seek additional mentoring, expert advice, and possibly even business partners to support your ventures.

That said, we believe sustaining success as an OBM Entrepreneur has eight components:

1. **A 1- to 3-year plan.** We will cover this more in the next chapter; however, the very nature of a plan is to have constant focus on your tangible goals to achieve in the short timeline of 1 year to no more than 3 years.

2. **Learning from failures and evolving quickly.** Failures, small or large, are essential to learn and achieve success. Integrating project look-back reviews, quarterly reviews of your business performance, client feedback, and planning to improve from failures will be essential to the success of the OBM Entrepreneur.

3. **Shaping toward ultimate goal—it takes time.** You may have a product or service idea you want to develop, but time and resources may not be abundant at the time. We believe in taking a shaping approach toward your ultimate goal, whether it be a product or service line, revenue or profit goals, or client-based goals.

4. **Maintaining those relationships.** We can't stress this component enough. OBM is a people business, and the OBM Entrepreneur destined for success maintains relationships, new ones, and long-term ones. From friends to colleagues to clients, don't lose sight of the power of maintaining relationships.

5. **Business fundamentals.** Know business fundamentals, such as LLC versus S Corporation, revenue, profit & loss, budgets, forecasting, lead generation and pipeline, operating costs, taxes—paying taxes and sales tax for the products you sell.

6. **OBM as the core.** One of most important things for the OBM Entrepreneur's success is to never forget what's at the core of the work and practice. OBM practitioners welcome other disciplines into their practice, and this should, in our opinion, continue. With OBM as the core, you will be ensuring a scientific approach to maximizing results for businesses.

7. **Vigilance in knowing your client base and competition.** We believe in taking an ongoing, active approach to knowing your client base and competition. Regular reviews of the demographics of your clients, who you're trying to attract, and the competitive landscape will be advantageous to your venture.

8. **Financial stability.** We cannot stress this enough. The OBM Entrepreneur will be served best by evaluating financial needs and making efforts to secure stability, whether it is through savings or lines of credit. Whether you're bootstrapping your business, starting with a loan, or taking on an investor, financial stability is critical, and we regularly seek advice from financial advisors.

Define the elements of relationship management

Write down 5 names of people you are working to either establish a relationship, define a relationship, manage a relationship, or evolve a relationship with. This should be seen as the beginning of a full list which will take some time to create but helps organize your behavior towards your relationship management efforts.

Name	Contact information	How we met?	Next steps

Identify the various roles and responsibilities of an OBM practitioner

Your Consulting Roles and Responsibilities Exercise: Now it's your turn. We want you to identify projects in which you are engaged in one or more of the roles and responsibilities we described: SME, Project Champion, Collaborator.

Project	SME	Champion	Collaborator
-	-	-	-
-		-	-
-	-	-	-

MY NOTES

ETHICS AND THE OBM
PRACTITIONER

Photo by Aleksandar Pasaric from Pexels

I saved this section for last as it is my intention to bring a fundamental set of ethical guidelines to the field of OBM and the practitioners who call themselves OBMers (OBM practitioners). Several pioneers in our field have described ethical considerations in our practice and some thought leadership on the notion of a certified professional in OBM (Bourdon, 1983; Parrott et al., 1983). Over the years, a fair amount has been written in regard to ethics in business from various perspectives—for instance from the *business and leadership perspective* (Bello, 2012; Brown et al., 2005; Daniels & Daniels, 2007; Solomon, 2004; Trevino, 1986), *a behavioral/psychological perspective* (Huhtala et al., 2014; Lattal & Clark, 2007), *the practice of behavior analysis* (Broadhead et al., 2018; Freeman et al., 2020;

Romanczyk, 2017; Sellers et al., 2016), and *OBM practitioners* specifically (Krapfl & Kruja, 2015; Luke et al., 2018; Mawhinney, 1984; Rodriguez et al., 2016). And over the years, I have consulted on, written about, and educated on OBM practice and research. Upon reflection and delving into certifications, I wanted to ensure ethics was part of the foundation for OBM practitioners. This goal may seem obvious, but far too often ethics is missing in the conversation and literature of OBM.

OBM and Ethics

When considering ethics and the OBM practitioner's role, the most recent body of work on the subject comes from Dr. Nicholas Weatherly (2021), who wrote the journal article "The Ethics of Organizational Behavior Management." Weatherly's focus on the ethical practice and decision-making of the OBM practitioner highlights several key elements. First, I really appreciated his point that "regardless of whether an individual is credentialed by a professional organization, any practitioner in any field should work to find some sort of ethical guidelines to help steer their professionalism." In *OBM Applied!* Volume 4, my colleagues, and I described *guiding principles for the OBM practitioner* (Rodriguez et al., 2016). In similar form to Weatherly's notion of ethical guidelines, we believed that "*adopting a set of principles helps ensure an effective and ethical practice*" (p. 30). The guiding principles for the OBM practitioner are illustrated here based on the work from Rodriguez et al. (2016).

The Client	The Science	The Impact
1. The "answer" to complex problems lies between you and your client. 2. Encourage and recognize diverse values and perspectives. 3. When working with your client, start from where they are now. 4. There is no blame; there is only resolve. 5. Do what you say you are going to do.	1. "Cookie cutter" is not science. 2. Self-management. 3. Come to the project with a basic consultation framework in mind. 4. Give and receive feedback. 5. Tracking, reviewing, and reporting data. 6. Consulting by walking around. 7. Keep it simple	1. Results, results, results. 2. Impact comes from not just what you do, but also how you do it. 3. It is up to your client to use, or not use, your advice. 4. Social significance. 5. Focus on what matters to everyone in the room. 6. Ethics check.

6. Know you are an instrument of change. 7. "Because I said so" is not a sufficient explanation. 8. Do not take it personally. 9. Always consult with the senior leader.	8. Behavior evokes behavior 9. Learning is happening 10. Terminology matters (but don't lose them in it!)	

An Illustration of the Guiding Principles for the OBM Practitioner (Rodriguez et al., 2016).

Supporting these guiding principles can be more specific ethical guidelines or even codes of ethics. The Society for Performance Improvement (ISPI; 2015) has a code of ethics for their members, certified performance improvement practitioners, specifically. The ISPI code of ethics is based on six principles: add value, validated practice, collaboration, continuous improvement, integrity, and upholding confidentiality. Weatherly (2021) described how OBM "relies on practitioners and researchers working together to build and apply proven OBM tools and services," which demonstrates a link between ISPI's code of ethics on collaboration and validated practice. Weatherly further described how advancements in OBM come from the "parameters of organizational, field and community standards...ethical standards help ensure practicing behavior analysts strategically pursue targeted results without sacrificing ethical or legal integrity." These points surely mirror the elements that ISPI (2015) suggests regarding the principles of adding value, integrity, and continuous improvement.

Behavior Analysts and Ethics

Weatherly (2021) chose to focus on the Behavior Analyst Certification Board's Professional and Ethical Compliance Code for Behavior Analysis (Behavior Analyst Certification Board, 2014). At the time of this work, being an OBM practitioner does not require a professional certification, including those offered by the Behavior Analyst Certification Board. Additionally, many OBM practitioners do not commonly obtain the BACB credentials. However, as Weatherly highlighted, "this does not mean that OBM practice cannot benefit from an ethical foundation for quality-control."

Weatherly described relevant codes applicable to the OBM practitioner given OBM's roots in behavior analysis. Supporting the use of a code helps practitioners and consumers of OBM services guide decision making. In summary, Weatherly (2021) suggested ethical decision-making for the OBM practitioner should do the following:

1. Remain reliant on scientific knowledge (BACB code element 1.01)
2. Appear competent in their practice and maintain boundaries related to their competency (BACB code element 1.02 and 1.03)
3. Demonstrate a high degree of Integrity (BACB code element 1.04)
4. Avoid and resolve conflicts of Interest (BACB code element 1.06)
5. Uphold their responsibility to clients (BACB code area 2.0)
   a. Accepting clients only if they have the proper training and mentorship (2.01)
   b. Maintaining records in accordance with laws, regulations, and policies (2.07)
   c. Ensuring behavior analytic solutions meet the needs of the client (2.09)
   d. Providing contracts, fees, and fiscal arrangements transparently and ensuring understanding (2.12)
   e. Avoiding any disruptions of service (2.15)
6. Conduct assessments to provide function-based solutions (BACB code element 3.01)
7. Present OBM assessments and solutions in understandable and actionable ways (BACB code element 3.04)
8. Maintain consistency with the principles of behavior (BACB code element 4.01)
9. Engage clients and internal personnel, and seek consent to move forward (BACB code element 4.02)
10. Assess environmental conditions that could interfere with the implementation of OBM solutions (BACB code element 4.07)
11. Use a least-restrictive alternative likely to be effective (BACB code element 4.09)
12. When acting as a supervisor (BACB code area 5.0)
    a. Supervise in area of competency (5.01)
    b. Maintain a volume of supervisees that ensures your effectiveness as a supervisor (5.02)
    c. Delegate tasks to supervisees based on their abilities (5.03)
    d. Communicate with supervisees about the supervision conditions (5.05)
5. Promote behavior analysis through dissemination (BACB code element 6.02)

6. Promote an ethical culture in the work environments (BACB code element 7.01)
7. When making public statements about OBM (BACB code area 8.0)
   a. Avoid false or deceptive statements (8.01)
   b. Respect intellectual property of others (8.02)
   c. Work with others to ensure the same (8.03)
   d. Avoid biased testimonials from current clients (8.05)
5. Avoid plagiarism, following appropriate laws and regulation, confidentiality, use of data, etc. (BACB code area 9.0)
   a. Disseminate research outcomes and procedures appropriately (9.02)

Ethical Guidelines for the OBM Practitioner

Photo by SevenStorm JUHASZIMRUS from Pexels

Considering all the great work before this book and respecting current OBM practitioners are all over the world, I decided the final piece for the OBM practitioner is a set of ethical guidelines. Not rules. Not a code. But guidelines to consider in their practice. Devising these guidelines was no easy feat. I had to consider my own history with ethics, my own behavior, and my current and future journey as an OBM practitioner. With much respect, I am hopeful these guidelines, outlined below, will serve you well.

Ethical Guidelines 1.0. Maintain Our Roots

"OBM is an application of behavior analysis" (Weatherly, 2021, p. 4).

1. OBM practitioners are respectful of the concepts and principles of behavior analysis.
2. OBM practitioners are focused on the seven dimensions of behavior analysis.
3. OBM practitioners are actively seeking applied research for evidence-based approaches.

Ethical Guidelines 2.0. People, Process, and Systems

"People do what they do, good or bad, because it works" (Weatherly, 2021, p. 2).

1. OBM practitioners engage with stakeholders at all levels.
2. OBM practitioners attend to organizational processes to enable performance.
3. OBM practitioners consider environmental factors within and outside (external) the organization.

Ethical Guidelines 3.0. Determining Success

"The success of OBM should be judged in a way that extends beyond our ability to get results" (Weatherly, 2021, p. 2).

1. OBM practitioners seek to define how success will be determined and how it will be measured.
2. OBM practitioners take a holistic approach to determining success beyond the bottom line, including via behavior change, culture change, and the integrity of solution implementation.
3. OBM practitioners evaluate the impact of behavior change and OBM solutions on those involved—employees, managers, executives, customers, and others.

Ethical Guidelines 4.0. Professionalism

"The point of scientific practice and research in OBM is to benefit the businesses, consumers, stakeholders, and others for whom the science is designed to benefit." (Weatherly, 2021, p. 11).

1. OBM practitioners maintain professional boundaries with clients, colleagues, and other professionals they work with directly or indirectly.
2. OBM practitioners ensure transparency in their practice with clients and colleagues.
3. OBM practitioners disseminate their work with clarity and integrity.
4. OBM practitioners demonstrate respect and concern for others at all times.
5. OBM practitioners hold themselves accountable to their work with clients, colleagues, and the field at large.

REFERENCES

Abernathy, W. B. (1996). *The sin of wages: Where the conventional pay system has led us and how to find a way out.* PerfSys Press.

Abernathy, W. B. (2011). *Pay for profit: Designing an organization-wide performance-based compensation system.* Performance Management Publications.

Abernathy, W. B. (2014). *The liberated workplace: Transitioning to walden three.* Performance Management Publications.

Agnew, J., & Daniels, A. (2010). *Safe by accident? Take the luck out of safety. leadership practices that a build sustainable safety culture.* Performance Management Publications.

Alexander, M. (2020). What is project scope? Defining and outlining project success. CIO.com. https://www.cio.com/article/3542776/what-is-project-scope-defining-and-outlining-project-success.html

Alvero, A. M., Bucklin, B. R., & Austin, J. (2001). An objective review of the effectiveness and essential characteristics of performance feedback in organizational settings. *Journal of Organizational Behavior Management, 21*(1), 3–29. http://dx.doi.org/10.1300/J075v21n01_02

Arnold, D., Edwards, M., Magruder, O., & Moore, S. (2019). *The competencies and goals of instructional designers: A survey study.* University Professional and Continuing Education Association. https://upcea.edu/wpcontent/uploads/2018/04/The-Competencies-and-Goals-of-Instructional-Designers-ASurvey-Study.pdf

Ashkenas, R., & Khan, R. (2014, May 30). You can't delegate change management. *Harvard Business Review.* https://hbr.org/2014/05/you-cant-delegate-change-management

Austin, J. (2000). Performance analysis and performance diagnostics. In J. Austin & J. E. Carr (Eds.), *Handbook of applied behavior analysis* (pp. 321–349). Context Press.

Austin, J, & Carr, J. E. (Eds.). (2000). *Handbook of applied behavior analysis*. Context Press.

Austin, J., Carr, J., & Agnew, J. L. (1999). Need for assessing maintaining variables in OBM. *Journal of Organizational Behavior Management, 19*, 59–87. https://doi.org/10.1300/J075v19n02_05

Baer, D. Wolf, M., & Risley, T. R. (1968). Some current dimensions of applied behavior analysis. *Journal of Applied Behavior Analysis, 1*(1), 91–97. https://dx.doi.org/10.1901%2Fjaba.1968.1-91

Behavior Analyst Certification Board. (2014). *Professional and ethical compliance code for behavior analysts.* https://www.bacb.com/wp-content/uploads/BACBCompliance-Code-english_190318.pdf

Bernstein, E. S. (2017). Making transparency transparent: The evolution of observation in management theory. *Academy of Management Annals, 11*(1), 217–266. https://doi.org/10.5465/annals.2014.0076

Binder, C. (1996). Behavioral fluency: Evolution of a new paradigm. *The Behavior Analyst, 19*(2), 163–197. https://dx.doi.org/10.1007%2FBF03393163

Binder, C. (2016). Integrating organizational-cultural values with performance management. *Journal of Organizational Behavior Management, 36*(2–3), 185–201. https://doi.org/10.1080/01608061.2016.1200512

Binder, C. (2017). What it really means to be accomplishment based. *Performance Improvement, 56*(4), 20–25. https://doi.org/10.1002/pfi.21702

Blanchard, K., & Bowles, S. (2004). Raving fans: Revolutionary approach to customer service. HarperCollins Publishers. (Original work published 1993).

Block, P. (1999). *Flawless consulting: A guide to getting your expertise used* (2nd ed.). Pfeiffer.

Boudon, R. D. (1983). The case against OBM certification: A reply to Parrott, Mitchell, and Gasparotto cost and benefits of certification for organizational behavior managers. *Journal of Organizational Behavior Management, 5*(2), 89–93. https://psycnet.apa.org/doi/10.1300/J075v05n02_06

Braksick, L. W. (2007). *Unlock behavior, unleash profits: Developing leadership behavior that drives profitability in your organization.* McGraw-Hill.

Brethower, D. M. (1972). *Behavior analysis in business and industry: A total performance system.* Behaviordelia.

Brethower, D. M. (1982). The total performance system. In R. O'Brien, A. Dickinson, & M. Rosow (Eds.), *Industrial behavior modification* (pp. 250–369). Pergamon.

Brethower, D. M. (1995). Specifying a human performance technology knowledgebase. *Performance Improvement Quarterly, 8*(2), 17–39. https://doi.org/10.1111/j.1937-8327.1995.tb00670.x

Brethower, D. M. (1999). General systems theory and behavioral psychology. In H.D. Stolovitch & E. J. Keeps (Eds.), *Handbook of human performance technology: Improving individual and organizational performance worldwide* (pp. 67–81). Jossey-Bass.

Brethower, D. M. (2000). A systematic view of enterprise: Adding value to performance. *Journal of Organizational Behavior Management, 20*(3–4), 165–190. https://psycnet.apa.org/doi/10.1300/J075v20n03_06

Brethower, D. M. (2001). Managing a person as a system. In L. J. Hayes, J. Austin, R. Houmanfar, & M. C. Clayton (Eds.), *Organizational change* (pp. 89–105). Context.

Brethower, D. M. (2008). Historical background for HPT certification standard 2, take a systems view, part 1. *Performance Improvement, 47*(2), 16–22. https://doi.org/10.1002/pfi.183

Brethower, D. M., & Dams, P. (1999). Systems thinking (and systems doing). *Performance Improvement, 38*(1), 37–51. https://doi.org/10.1002/pfi.4140380109

Brown, A. S. (2005, September 13). *The charter: Selling your project* [Paper presentation]. PMI® Global Congress 2005—North America, Toronto, Ontario,

Canada, Newtown Square, PA. https://www.pmi.org/learning/library/charter-selling-project-7473

Brown, P. (1982). *Managing behavior on the job*. John Wiley & Sons.

Bucklin, B., Rodriguez, M., & Eagle, L. (2020, June). Pay for performance. *Business Science Magazine*.

Carr, J. E., Wilder, D. A., Majdalany, L., Mathisen, D., & Strain, L. (2013). An assessment-based solution to a human-service employee performance problem: An initial evaluation of the Performance Diagnostic Checklist–Human Services. *Behavior Analysis in Practice*, *6*, 16–32. https://dx.doi.org/10.1007%2FBF03391789

Chavez, M. (2019, April 22). *The power of purpose in projects*. Forbes. https://www.forbes.com/sites/michaelchavez/2019/04/22/the-power-of-purpose-in-projects/?sh=7cbf6db15344

Clow, J. (2012). *The work revolution: Freedom and excellent for all*. Wiley.

Daniels, A. C. (1989). *Performance management: Improving quality productivity through positive reinforcement* (2nd ed.). Performance Management Publications.

Daniels, A. C. (2001). *Other people's habits*. McGraw-Hill.

Daniels, A. C., & Bailey, J. S. (2014). *Performance management: Changing behavior that drives organizational effectiveness* (6th ed.). Performance Management Publications.

Daniels, A. (2015, January 13). *Measurement: Friend or foe?* Aubrey Daniels International. https://www.aubreydaniels.com/blog/2015/01/13/measurement-friend-foe

Daniels, A. C. (2016). *Bringing out the best in people: How to apply the astonishing power of positive reinforcement* (3rd ed.). McGraw-Hill Education.

Daniels, A. C., & Daniels, J. E. (2007). *Measure of a leader: The legendary leadership formula for producing exceptional performers and outstanding results*. McGraw-Hill Education.

Daniels, A. C., & Bailey, J. E. (2014). *Performance management: Improving quality productivity through positive reinforcement* (5th ed.). Performance Management Publications.

Dickinson (2001). The historical roots of organizational behavior management in the private sector. *Journal of Organizational Behavior Management, 20*(3-4), 9–58. https://doi.org/10.1300/J075v20n03_02

Dickinson, A. M., & Poling, A. (1996). Schedules of monetary reinforcement in organizational behavior management. *Journal of Organizational Behavior Management, 16*(1), 71–91. https://doi.org/10.1300/J075v16n01_05

Ditzian, K., Wilder, D., King, A., & Tanz, J. (2015). An evaluation of the Performance Diagnostic Checklist–Human Services to assess an employee performance problem in a center-based autism treatment facility. *Journal of Applied Behavior Analysis, 48*, 199–203. https://doi.org/10.1002/jaba.171

Duncan, P. K., & Bruwelheide, L. R. (1986). Feedback: Use and possible behavioral functions. *Journal of Organizational Behavior Management, 7*(3–4), 91–114. https://psycnet.apa.org/doi/10.1300/J075v07n03_06

Freeman, T. R., LeBlanc, L. A., & Martinez-Diaz, J. A. (2020). Ethical and professional responsibilities of applied behavior analysts. In J. O. Cooper, T. E. Heron, & W. L. Heward (Eds.), *Applied behavior analysis* (3rd ed., p. 759). Person Education.

Gavoni, P., & Rodriguez, M. (2016). *Quick wins! Accelerating school transformation through science, engagement, and leadership.* ABA Technologies.

Gavoni, P., & Weatherly, N. (2018). *Deliberate coaching: A toolbox for accelerating teacher performance.* Learning Sciences International.

Geller, E. S. (2000). *The psychology of safety handbook.* Lewis Publishers.

Geller, E. S. (2001). *Working safe: How to help people actively care for health and safety* (2nd ed.). Lewis Publishers.

Geller, E. S. (2003). Should organizational behavior management expand its content? *Journal of Organizational Behavior Management, 22*(2), 13–30. https://doi.org/10.1300/J075v22n02_03

Gershon, D. (2007). Changing behavior in organizations: The practice of empowerment. *Systems Thinker*, *17*(10). https://thesystemsthinker.com/changing-behavior-in-organizations-the-practice-of-empowerment/

Gilbert, T. F. (1978). *Human competence: Engineering worthy performance.* McGraw-Hill.

Giles, S. (2016, March 15). The most important leadership competencies, according to leaders around the world. *Harvard Business Review.* https://hbr.org/2016/03/the-mostimportant-leadership-competencies-according-to-leaders-around-the-world

Gligorea, R. (2013, June 14). Avoiding the balanced scorecard pitfalls. *Performance Magazine.* https://www.performancemagazine.org/avoiding-the-balanced-scorecard-pitfalls/

Gravina, N., Cummins, B., & Austin, J. (2017). Leadership's role in process safety: An understanding of behavioral science among managers is needed. *Journal of Organizational Behavior Management, 37*(3–4), 316–331. https://doi.org/10.1080/01608061.2017.1340925

Greenleaf R. (2007). The servant as leader. In W. C. Zimmerli, M. Holzinger, & K. Richter (Eds.), *Corporate ethics and corporate governance.* Heidelberg. https://doi.org/10.1007/978-3-540-70818-6_6

Hantula, D. A. (2001). Schedules of reinforcement in organizational performance, 1971–1994: Application, analysis, and synthesis. In C. M. Johnson, W. K. Redmon, & T. C. Mawhinney (Eds.), *Handbook of organizational performance: Behavior analysis and management* (pp. 139–166). Haworth Press.

Hayes, L. J., Austin, J., Houmanfar, R., & Clayton, M. C. (2001). *Organizational change.* Context Press.

Hopkins, B., & Mawhinney, T. (Eds.). (1992). *Pay for performance: History, controversy, and evidence.* Hawthorne Press.

Hyten, C. (2009). Strengthening the focus on business results: The need for systems approaches in organizational behavior management. *Journal of Organizational Behavior Management, 29*(2), 87–107. http://dx.doi.org/10.1080/01608060902874526

Johnson, C. M., Redmon, W. K., & Mawhinney, T. C. (2001). *Handbook of organizational performance: Behavior analysis and management.* Haworth Press.

Johnson, D. A., Casella, S. E., McGee, H., & Lee, S. C. (2014). The use and validation of preintervention diagnostic tools in organizational behavior management. *Journal of Organizational Behavior Management, 34*(2), 104–121. https://doi.org/10.1080/01608061.2014.914009

Kaplan, R. S., & Norton, D. (1992). The balanced scorecard: Measures that drive performance. *Harvard Business Review, 70*(1), 71–79.

Kaplan, R. S., & Norton, D. P. (1996). Linking the balanced scorecard to strategy. *California Management Review, 39*(1), 53–79. https://doi.org/10.2307%2F41165876

Katzenbach, J. R., Steffen, I., & Kronley, C. (2012). Cultural change that sticks: Start with what's already working. *Harvard Business Review, 90*(7–8):110–117, 162.

Komaki, J., Blood, M., & Holder, D. (1980). Fostering friendliness in a fast food franchise. *Journal of Organizational Behavior Management, 2*(3), 151–164. https://doi.org/10.1300/J075v02n03_02

Kotter, J. (2012). *Leading change* (1R ed.). Harvard Business Review Press.

Krapfl, J. E. & Kruja, B. (2015). Leadership and culture. *Journal of Organizational Behavior Management, 35*(1–2), 28–43. https://doi.org/10.1080/01608061.2015.1031431

Latham, G. P., & Huber, V. L. (1991). Schedules of reinforcement: Lessons from the past and issues for the future. *Journal of Organizational Behavior Management, 12*(1), 125–149. https://doi.org/10.1300/J075v12n01_06

Lattal, A. D., & Clark, R. W. (2007). *A good day's work: Sustaining ethical behavior and business success.* McGraw-Hill.

Lattal, D. (2013, March). Ethical decision making in the workplace. *Performance Management Publications, 17*(4). https://www.aubreydaniels.com/sites/default/files/Editorial.Ethical%20Decision%20Making%20in%20the%20Workplace.PMM_.17.4.pdf

Llopis, G. (2012). *5 powerful things happen when a leader is transparent.* Forbes. https://www.forbes.com/sites/glennllopis/2012/09/10/5-powerful-things-happen-when-a-leader-is-transparent/?sh=5ce3b9d54a3a

Lucid Meetings (2020). *What is a 2x2 matrix?* https://www.lucidmeetings.com/glossary/2x2-matrix

Ludwig, T. D., & Frazier, C. B. (2012). Employee engagement and organizational behavior management. *Journal of Organizational Behavior Management, 32,* 75–82. https://doi.org/10.1080/01608061.2011.619439

Luke, M. M., Carr, J. E., & Wilder, D. A. (2018). On the compatibility of organizational behavior management and BACB certification. *Journal of Organizational Behavior Management, 38*(4), 288–305. https://doi.org/10.1080/01608061.2018.1514347

Luthans, F., & Kreitner, R. (1975). *Organizational behavior modification.* Scott Foresman.

Mager, R. F., & Pipe, P. (1970). *Analyzing performance problems.* Fearon.

Malott, M. E. (2003). *Paradox of organizational change: Engineering organizations with behavioral systems analysis.* Context Press.

Malott, R. W. (1992). A theory of rule-governed behavior and organizational behavior management. *Journal of Organizational Behavior Management, 12*(2), 45–65. https://psycnet.apa.org/doi/10.1300/J075v12n02_03

Marr, B. (2016, June 14). *Data-driven decision making: 10 simple steps for any business.* Forbes. https://www.forbes.com/sites/bernardmarr/2016/06/14/data-driven-decision-making-10-simple-steps-for-any-business/#65cb15845e1e

Mawhinney, T. C. (1984). Philosophical and ethical aspects of organizational behavior management. *Journal of Organizational Behavior Management, 6*(1), 5–31. https://psycnet.apa.org/doi/10.1300/J075v06n01_02

Mawhinney, T. (1992). *Organizational culture, rule-governed behavior, and organizational behavior management: Theoretical foundations and implications for research and practice.* Hawthorne Press.

McSween, T. (2003). *The value-based safety process* (2nd ed.). John Wiley & Sons.

Norreklit, H., Jacobsen, M., & Mitchell, F. (2008). Pitfalls in using the balanced scorecard. *Corporate Accounting and Finance, 19*(6), 65–68. https://doi. org/10.1002/jcaf.20436

O'Brien, R. M., Dickinson, A. M., & Rosow, M. P. (Eds.) (1982). *Industrial behavior modification: A management handbook.* Pergamon Press.

Pampino, R., Heering, P., Wilder, D. A., Barton, C., & Burson, L. (2003). The use of the Performance Diagnostic Checklist to guide intervention selection in an independently owned coffee shop. *Journal of Organizational Behavior Management, 23*(2), 5–19. https://psycnet.apa.org/doi/10.1300/ J075v23n02_02

Parks, N., Tudor, A., & Ventura, A. (2020). *Leadership in behavior analysis: The independent variable that advances our field.* 305 Publishing.

Parrott, L. J., Mitchell, V., & Gasparotto, G. (1983). Costs and benefits of certification for organizational behavior managers. *Journal of Organizational Behavior Management, 5*(1), 63–73. https://doi.org/10.1300/J075v05n01_07

Parsons, H. M. (1991) Hawthorne: An early OBM experiment. *Journal of Organizational Behavior Management, 12*(1), 27–43. https://doi.org/10.1300/ J075v12n01_03

Pathak, R. (2020, July 9). *Top 5 project management phases.* Project-Management. com. https://project-management.com/project-management-phases/

Project Management Institute. (2020). *What is project management?* https://www. pmi.org/about/learn-about-pmi/what-is-project-management

Prosci. (2020). An introduction to change management: What it is and why it makes a difference in your organization (2020). https://www.prosci.com/ resources/articles/the-what-why-and-how-of-change-management

Prue, D. M., Frederiksen, L. W., & Bacon, A. (1978). Organizational behavior management: An annotated bibliography. *Journal of Organizational Behavior Management, 1*(4), 216–257. https://doi.org/10.1300/J075v01n04_01

Quinn, R. W., & Quinn, R. E. (2016, January 7). Change management and leadership development have to mesh. *Harvard Business Review.*

https://hbr.org/2016/01/change-management-and-leadership-development-have-to-mesh

Robbins, T. (2019). *Creating raving fan customers: Raving fans are your pipeline for future loyal customers.* https://www.tonyrobbins.com/career-business/create-raving-fan-customers/

Robinson, D. (2018). *What core competencies do performance consultants need?* Association for Talent Development. https://www.td.org/insights/what-core-competencies-do-performance-consultants-need

Rodriguez, M. A. (2011). Cash is king—How OBM helped a North American telecommunications organization obtain $76 million in receivables. *Journal of Organizational Behavior Management, 31*(3), 163–178. https://doi.org/10.1080/01608061.2011.589733

Rodriguez, M. (2016, February). *10 ways OBMers do it! Behavioral science of the 21ˢᵗ century.* Behavior Science in the 21st Century. www.bsci21.org

Rodriguez, M. (2018). The 5 P's of an OBM project. *Chief Motivating Officers.* https://www.chiefmotivatingofficers.com/5ps-obm

Rodriguez, M., & Biagi, S. (2018, June 19). *An OBM perspective on the task list.* Behavioral Science of the 21ˢᵗ Century. https://bsci21.org/an-obm-perspective-onthe-task-list/

Rodriguez, M. (2019, September). Don't forget the "M" in project management. *Business Science Magazine.*

Rodriguez, M., & Parks, N. (2019). *OBM entrepreneur: Launching your OBM practice.* 305 Publishing, Miami, FL: USA.

Rodriguez, M. (2020, May). Empowering others. *Business Science Magazine,* 5–7.

Rodriguez, M. (2020). *Identifying effective systems and processes to promote ethical workplace cultures in the applied behavior analysis (ABA) therapy industry* [Doctoral dissertation, University of South Florida]. USF Scholar Commons. https://scholarcommons.usf.edu/etd/8483

Rodriguez, M., Sundberg, D., & Biagi, S. (2016a). *OBM applied! A practical guide to implementing organizational behavior management: Vol. 1. Setting the stage for improving performance.* ABA Technologies.

Rodriguez, M., Sundberg, D., & Biagi, S. (2016b). *OBM applied! A practical guide to implementing organizational behavior management: Vol. 2. Choosing the right solution.* ABA Technologies.

Rodriguez, M., Sundberg, D., & Biagi, S. (2016c). *OBM applied! A practical guide to implementing organizational behavior management: Vol. 3. Making a positive difference.* ABA Technologies.

Rodriguez, M., Sundberg, D., & Biagi, S. (2016d). *OBM applied! A practical guide to implementing organizational behavior management: Vol. 4. Creating lasting change.* ABA Technologies.

Rodriguez, M., Wilder, D. A., Therrien, K., Wine, B., Miranti, R., Daratany, K., Salume, G., Baranovsky, G., & Rodriguez, M. (2006). Use of the Performance Diagnostic Checklist to select an intervention designed to increase the offering of promotional stamps at two sites of a restaurant franchise. *Journal of Organizational Behavior Management, 25*(3), 17–35. https://psycnet.apa.org/doi/10.1300/J075v25n03_02

Romanczyk, R. G. (2017). Ethical and competent practice in applied behavior analysis: perspective, requirements, and dilemmas. In J. E. Luiselli (Ed.), *Applied behavior analysis advanced guidebook: A manual for professional practice* (1st ed.). Elsevier.

Rummler, G. A., & Brache, A. P. (1995). *Improving performance: How to manage the white space on the organization chart* (2nd ed.). Josscy-Bass.

RummlerBrache (2020). Overcoming the Seven Deadly Sins of Process Improvement. Free Article, RummlerBrache Group, Retrieved April 28, 2021, https://www.rummlerbrache.com/overcoming-seven-deadly-sins-process-improvement-0

Seidman, I. (2013). *Interview as qualitative research: A guide for researchers in education and the social sciences* (4th ed.). Teachers College Press.

Schedule of reinforcement [Image]. (2020). Wikimedia Commons. Retrieved June 8, 2020, from https://commons.wikimedia.org/wiki/File:Schedule_of_reinforcement.png

Smith, J. (2002). *It happens: How to become change-resilient.* Life Path Press.

Spillane, J. P. (2012). Data in practice: Conceptualizing the data-based decision-making phenomena. *American Journal of Education, 118*(2), 113–141. https://doi.org/10.1086/663283

Sulzer-Azaroff, B. (1998). *Who killed my daddy?* Cambridge Center for Behavioral Studies.

Therrien, K., & Rodriguez, M. (2007). OBM—The next generation. *OBM Network Newsletter, 21*(1), 14–17.

Thomas, K. (2004). *Coaching for change: Practical strategies for transforming performance.* Kogan Page.

Tilka, R., & Johnson, D. A. (2018). Coaching as a packaged intervention for telemarketing personnel. *Journal of Organizational Behavior Management, 38*(1), 49–72. https://doi.org/10.1080/01608061.2017.1325821

Vroom, V. H., & Jago, A. G. (2007). The role of the situation in leadership. *American Psychologist, 62*(1), 17–24. http://dx.doi.org/10.1037/0003-066X.62.1.17

Weatherly, N. (2021). The ethics of organizational behavior management. *Journal of Organizational Behavior Management.* https://doi.org/10.1080/01608061.2021.1890664

Weiss, M. J., Gatzunis, K., & Aljohani, W. (2021). How to integrate multiculturalism and diversity sensitivity into the training and ethical skill set of behavior analysts. In B. Conners & S. T. Capell (Eds.), *Multiculturalism and diversity in applied behavior analysis: Bridging theory and application* (1st ed.). Routledge

Wilder, D. A., Lipschultz, J., & Gehrman, C. (2018). An evaluation of the Performance Diagnostic Checklist—Human Services (PDC–HS) across domains. *Behavior Analysis in Practice, 11*, 129–138. https://doi.org/10.1007/s40617-018-0243-y

Wilk, L. A., & Redmon, W. K. (1998). The effects of feedback and goals setting on the productivity and satisfaction of university admissions staff. *Journal of Organizational Behavior Management*, 18, 45–68. https://doi.org/10.1300/J075v18n01_04

Yi, H., Hao, P., Yang, B., & Liu, W. (2017). How leaders' transparent behavior influences employee creativity: The mediating roles of psychological safety and ability to focus attention. *Journal of Leadership & Organizational Studies*, 24(3), 335–344. https://doi.org/10.1177%2F1548051816670306

ABOUT THE AUTHOR

Dr. Manuel "Manny" Rodriguez's career includes launching business consultancies, implementing strategic initiatives for Fortune 500 companies, and educating practitioners and leaders across the globe on the power of behavior science applied to business. Manny has worked with the consultancies Aubrey Daniels International and The Continuous Learning Group (now Alula), led strategic initiatives as a senior manager and executive for FMC Corporation, ACES, and ABA Technologies, and Co-founded several startup organizations. He has been invited as a keynote speaker at several national and international conferences and has authored articles on the subject of Organizational Behavior Management (OBM), leadership. performance management, and ethics. Manny co-authored the four volume book _"OBM Applied!,"_ co authored with Dr. Paul Gavoni the book _"Quick Wins!"_ and coauthored with Dr. Natalie Parks the book _"OBM Entrepreneur."_

Manny had the great honor of serving as President and Executive Director of the OBM Network, a non-profit organization which he helped grow to over 400 professionals. In addition, Manny has helped launch successful startups, provided direct consulting to small and large businesses, and has taught university coursework at over ten major colleges.

Manny received a dual bachelor's degree in criminology and psychology from Florida State University, a master's degree in Applied Behavior Analysis at the Florida Institute of Technology, and his Doctorate of Business Administration from the University of South Florida's MUMA College of Business. Currently Manny fills his day serving the role of Continuous Improvement Manager for Trenton Corporation based in Ann Arbor Michigan, and is CEO of Bueno Ventures Management Services, a business consultancy, and venture capital investment company. When he is not working, Manny enjoys his family time with his children, wife, dogs, fish, and the soccer and softball teams he coaches.